All Aboar
Poetry E

The East
& South Of England

Edited by
Donna Samworth

This book belongs to

First published in Great Britain in 2010 by

 Young**Writers**

Remus House
Coltsfoot Drive
Peterborough
PE2 9JX
Telephone: 01733 890066
Website: www.youngwriters.co.uk

Foreword

At Young Writers our defining aim is to promote an enjoyment of reading and writing amongst children and young adults. By giving aspiring poets the opportunity to see their work in print, their love of the written word as well as confidence in their own abilities has the chance to blossom.

Our latest competition *Poetry Express* was designed to introduce primary school children to the wonders of creative expression. They were given free reign to write on any theme and in any style, thus encouraging them to use and explore a variety of different poetic forms.

We are proud to present the resulting collection of regional anthologies which are an excellent showcase of young writing talent. With such a diverse range of entries received, the selection process was difficult yet very rewarding.

From comical rhymes to poignant verses, there is plenty to entertain and inspire within these pages. We hope you agree that this collection bursting with imagination is one to treasure.

Contents

Whatfield CE (VC) Primary School, Whatfield

Witnesham Primary School, Ipswich

The Poems

Fear

Fear looks like an angry black dog,
That never stops attacking.
The colour of fear is the colour of death,
Dark and deeply black.
Fear sounds like a group of people
Begging and screaming for mercy
The taste of blood running through my body,
That's been extracted from my heart.
Fear smells like a rotting trench,
That never ever stops rotting.
It looks like the beast from the depths of Hell,
That replaces your happiness with fear.
Fear can cause your blood to run cold
and may even drive you mad.
But there's one emotion that can conquer fear,
Hope!

Michael Nicholls (11)
Castle Hill Primary School, Croydon

Pain

Pain is sorrowful sounds of sheep
Being slaughtered by the fearless, frightening farmer.
It tastes like rotten sausages, cooked
By the cooks in the clutter of a kitchen.
Red is like fire burning
In the Great Fire of London.
Pain smells like blood dripping from an old carcass,
Living in the deep depths of the dungeon.
Pain feels like being stabbed in the back
By your friends.
You see vampires drifting through the midnight sky.
Pain reminds you of someone passing away.

Regan Roberts (10)
Castle Hill Primary School, Croydon

Pain

Pain tastes like fiery ribs of burning Hell,
Up in the misty skies, the screaming voice
Engulfed every bit of cloud!
It is like a black fading eagle,
Never stopping to catch my heart!
Pain is people at risk of serious danger,
Glorifying death!
The alarming scent of death, around the whole Earth
Down to the never-ending alleyway!
Pain is dark red as midnight depths!
The horrible food on the floor, littered all alone,
Ready to be devoured.
A room full of blood and veins,
Making me very anxious!
Pain actually feels like terror!

Danté Jones (11)
Castle Hill Primary School, Croydon

Pain

Pain is red, blood-red.
It tastes of burnt popcorn that has just come out of a metallic
microwave,
Pain sounds like someone being buried alive,
Inside a rotting coffin in a grave.
It looks like a werewolf being slaughtered
by the mysterious Grim Reaper, in the poisonous midnight air.
It is as sharp as the Devil's razor-sharp horns on the top of his head.
Pain smells like the rotten stench of burning souls,
Rising from the deep depths of Hell.
Pain reminds me of the dark red blood
Dripping down the wet, mossy wall.
Pain.

Brooke Murphy (11)
Castle Hill Primary School, Croydon

Terror

It sounds like the screech of metals rubbing against each other
And the screams of men, women and children and the starting of a
chainsaw.
It is that pitch-black shadow that always seems to follow you,
It is that dark room that you're afraid to be alone in.
It's that stench of blood and rotting corpses.
It's as dark as the night and as black as the midnight sky
In the deep, dark depths of the blackest shadow of Hell.
Terror is that boost of adrenaline that comes to you when terror
strikes!
Terror reminds me of a dead, pale white zombie from the dark depths
of Hell
With blood omitting from his blackened eyes
It reminds me of the one right behind me . . .

Kayun Huggins (11)
Castle Hill Primary School, Croydon

Terror!

Terror sounds like the deafening scream of souls
Being constantly burnt in *Hell!*
It looks like the dark red, deadly blood
Slowly running down both fangs of a vampire's teeth.
Terror also smells like the nauseating stench
Of dilapidating souls being sliced in half and left to rot.
It tastes like the revolting bile at the back of your throat.
When terror is around,
It feels like the cold misty air brushing rapidly
Against the tiny hairs on your skin,
As well as putting the hairs on the back of your neck on end.
Terror is *death!*

Natalee Barnett (11)
Castle Hill Primary School, Croydon

3

Livid

It tastes of the kisses you get from your granny.
It feels so dreadful;
It feels like your tongue is being cut out with a dagger.
Livid is such a horrific smell -
If one breath is inhaled, you die instantly.
It looks like rampaging grannies
Sprinting for the fridge section in Iceland.
The colour is like a dark mist that involves you when in a deep rage.
Livid is the deafening sound you get from thunder,
Causing cities and villages to scream in pain and horror.
It reminds you of . . . *death.*

Byron Ewart (11)
Castle Hill Primary School, Croydon

Love

Listen to the birds singing in the green trees,
The scent of freshly picked roses drifted below my nostrils,
Taste the sweet and sour strawberries,
Love is red and pink, just like a flying love pig,
Look at the hearts twinkling in time with the silver stars,
I feel so delightful right now,
It just reminds me of birdsong on a Friday night,
Love is special,
Love is pride,
When I'm with you,
I feel loved inside.

Shannon Collier (11)
Castle Hill Primary School, Croydon

Love

Love is the sound of gentle music blooming in the gentle breeze.
It tastes of strawberries smothered in cream
With melted chocolate on the top.
Love smells of freshly watered flowers
Waving around in the soft breeze.
Love looks like a gigantic love heart in the sky
Shining over everyone.
It feels like you have got all of your friends around you at once.
Love reminds me of birds singing
At the top of their voices in the treetops.

Jordan Callow (11)
Castle Hill Primary School, Croydon

Jealousy

Jealousy is a dishonest friend,
It feels as irritating as a knitted jumper,
Jealousy is the smell of rotting corpses,
Dying for freshly spilled blood,
It tastes of revolting, decayed eggs,
Jealousy sounds like ferocious roars from a pair of terrifying lions,
Fighting in a colossal arena,
Jealousy is a light purple that shines too bright for the naked eye,
Jealousy is a dark cave in the deep depths of nowhere,
Jealousy . . .

Ellie Shires (11)
Castle Hill Primary School, Croydon

A Love Poem

The sweet sound of children playing with their sisters or brothers.
While their mum and dad are watching them play.
The sound of them playing makes me feel like I am a child again.
The smell of red blossoming flowers on the tree
And the pink flowers on the floor make me happy.
I felt the flowers that made me want to sneeze
Because of all the love I have in my heart
And the sweet sound of the children playing made me hungry
So I went to get some lunch.

Chelsea Peters (10)
Castle Hill Primary School, Croydon

Pain

Pain sounds like children bellowing out from the room in horror,
It tastes of burnt black toast,
Which had been reheated thousands of times,
It reminds me of the Great Fire of London
When people ran for their lives,
Pain smells like the deep depths of the sewers,
Pain is as red as the blood,
Which drips slowly from the vampire's fangs.
Violence!

Amy Read (10)
Castle Hill Primary School, Croydon

Happiness

Happiness sounds like joy from happy children playing.
Happiness smells like red roses and freshly mown lawn.
Happiness tastes like freshly made McDonald's chips.
Happiness looks like the rainbow high in the sunny sky.

Daniel Palmer (11)
Castle Hill Primary School, Croydon

Terror

Terror sounds like the screams of a thousand souls
Bursting in my eardrums,
It's the sight of vampires feasting upon rotting corpses,
It's the liquid blood that engulfs those in pain,
It's the stench of rotten bodies rising from the graves,
It's the stars of a million souls examining you internally,
It reminds you of the Devil!

Lewis Hallam (11)
Castle Hill Primary School, Croydon

Sadness

Sadness, sadness sounds like a lonely child crying from the corner.
It feels like sorrow building up in my body mysteriously.
Sadness tastes of a lone tear trickling down my cheeks.
It looks like cold, wet tears running down my soft, stained cheeks.
The colour of sadness is as grey as a donkey's rough and rigid fur.
Sadness, sadness reminds me of people
Who have passed away in my life . . .

Aliza Naqvi (11)
Castle Hill Primary School, Croydon

Happiness Is . . .

Happiness is the sound of the waves
Crashing together as the heavy wind blows.
As blue as the opened up sky, swirling everywhere.
Happiness is the scent of rose petals
Being picked off of the bud.
As beautiful as a bunch of red roses.
Happiness is the touch of a really soft pillow.
As fluffy as warm, cosy fur . . .

Amelia Quint (9)
Fairfield Park Lower School, Stotfold

Happiness Feels Miraculous

Happiness feels miraculous, all bubbly inside
It churns you up,
It cheers you up yippee, yippee yi!
It is as shiny as a diamond, as polished as a trophy!
Happiness is a vibrant gold,
The opposite of cold!
It amazes you,
It crazes you, hey, hey, hey, hey, ho!
It is a banner of light as bright as sunshine.
Happiness is the sweet taste of sugar and strawberries
The magic couple!
It makes you feel speechless and cheatless, yes!
As tasty as sweeties!
Happiness smells like a fresh summer's day,
Not even a trace of smelly hay! Yay, yay!
It is a succulent rose!
As smelly as an air-freshener!

Beth Guiney (7)
Fairfield Park Lower School, Stotfold

Fun Is . . .

Fun is running around,
As happy as can be.
Fun is laughing out loud,
As strong as anyone can.
Fun is a yellow glow,
As bright as the morning sun.
Fun is the smell of flowers,
As sweet as a beautiful red heart.
Fun is touching your best friend,
As kindly as you like.

Daniel Lacy (7)
Fairfield Park Lower School, Stotfold

Excitement Is . . .

Excitement is a fresh smell,
As fresh as water,
Wet, washable water.

Excitement is a trickling waterfall,
Trickling as soft as a smooth cushion,
Splashing and sploshing.

Excitement is people laughing,
As happy as can be,
Laughing, laughing, laughing.

Excitement is a hand of water,
As wet as a wet river,
Helpful, handy hands.

The colour is blue
As blue as the deep sea,
Colourful colours.

Camryn Connolly (8)
Fairfield Park Lower School, Stotfold

Love

Love is a beautiful heart,
As lovely as a flower.
Love is a fresh rose,
As fragrant as an air-freshener.
Love is a delicate hug,
As cuddly as a kitten.
Love is a blue ocean,
As bright as the golden sun.
Love is a nice gentle humming,
As soft as the breeze.

Mia Quint (8)
Fairfield Park Lower School, Stotfold

Seeing Deeply Disappointed People Is . . .

A black thunder cloud rolling across the murderous ebony sky,
As sad as a rainy day.
Soaking, sad, sorry,
Feeling disappointed is a black pitch grain.
As moody as a bull.
Bad and bullied.
The colour of disappointment is black, a black devil.
As mad as a puppy.
Mad and moody.
Disappointment is the sound of crying and silence.
As silent as the deep blue sea.
Huge, deep and blue.
Disappointment is the smell of a gentle black fire.
As quiet as a trickling waterfall.
Slow, black and trickling.

Ellie Warwick (8)
Fairfield Park Lower School, Stotfold

Love Is . . .

Love is my sweet mummy,
As sweet as a bird's tweet
Sweet, sensitive but very stern.

Love is a cherry pie
As smelly as candyfloss.
Love is a warm hug,
As soft as a pillow.

Love is lipstick,
As creamy as the creamiest cream.
Love is the sound of hugging,
As lovely as a red rose.

What does love mean to you?

Megan Morton (8)
Fairfield Park Lower School, Stotfold

Surprise Is . . .

Surprise is people's mouths opening extremely wide
As wide as a door
Wonderful, wicked and wide.
Surprise is a special birthday cake
As nice as a lovely air-freshener
Sniffing smelly scents.
Surprise is opening a perfect present
As rough as bark
Rough, round and rocky.
Surprise is a lovely light blue
As blue as a blueberry
Beautiful blueberry.
Surprise is people shouting in excitement
As loud as a *boom, bang, boo, bang, boo!*

Clodiagh Johnston (8)
Fairfield Park Lower School, Stotfold

Fantastic Football Joy

Joy is like England in the final at football,
As exciting as a clown doing his ball skills
Which are superbly silly and slow skills!

Joy is like the smell of a stinky, soggy and seriously sweet football match
And the smell of the players that are ferociously stinky!

Joy is a mad bright red colour
Which glows as bright as the sun on steroids
So the sun stays so, so, so, so bright!

Joy is like a football
Signed by one of the most famous football players in the world
As good at football as a player made up all of Arsenal.

Myles Johnson (9)
Fairfield Park Lower School, Stotfold

11

Happiness

Happiness is a bright pink
As beautiful as a bright pink dress
Brilliant, beautiful and bright.

Happiness is working together.
Happiness is as exciting as a surprise,
Work, working and work's good.

Happiness is a romantic talk
As romantic as a delicate perfume,
Pretty, perfect, perfume.

Happiness is lovely laughter,
As lovely as can be.

Maddy Richardson (8)
Fairfield Park Lower School, Stotfold

Excitement

Excitement is like a boy screaming!
It is as funny as a clown.
It reminds me of somebody jumping up and down!
It is as mad as a puppy.
It is as sweet as a pineapple!
It is as sparkly as the stars.
Excitement is like something good is going to happen!
It is as fun as the funfair.
Excitement is like a red rose starting to grow!
It is as happy as your birthday.

Greg Seed (9)
Fairfield Park Lower School, Stotfold

Excitement Is . . .

Excitement is a happy fairground
As happy as a party.
Excitement is a birthday cake
As smelly as perfume.
Excitement is making a cake
As nice as a piece of cake.
Excitement is a colourful red rose
As colourful as a red rose.
Excitement is laughter.
Exciting is a birthday party.

Joshua Gibbs (7)
Fairfield Park Lower School, Stotfold

Happy Times

Fun is a happy secret laughing
As fun as watching CBBC while eating sweets and laughing
It is as fun as playing on a fairground ride
Also as excellent as a touch of a ticket.
It is as fun as finding golden coins at the end of the rainbow
As well as entering a rainbow-coloured land.
It is a violet rose smell,
While as nice as a sniff of fresh grass.
Fun is as fun as seeing huge dolphins splashing,
While it is as fun as seeing rainbows.

Alex Clarke (7)
Fairfield Park Lower School, Stotfold

Fun

Fun is a joyful fairground,
Just as fun as having a party.
Fun is the smell of cooking cakes,
As delicious as a bunch of biscuits.
Fun is a touch of hands at a wedding,
The hands feel as soft as kittens' fur.
Fun is the colour peach,
Because hands meet as peach as skin.
Fun is immense laughter,
As loud as a lion's roar.

Eleanor Farley (7)
Fairfield Park Lower School, Stotfold

My Emotion, Love . . .

Love is a red apple
Love is smooth as a baby's bottom!
Love is a flower blowing in the wind.
As gentle as a summer breeze!
Love is romantic music.
As romantic as a kiss!
Love is red
As red as a rose!
Love is a sensational perfume.
As sensational as a flower!

Charmaine Day (8)
Fairfield Park Lower School, Stotfold

What Is Excitement?

Excitement is a drink fizzing,
Excitement is running around in madness,
Crazy, cool and comical.

Excitement has a giggly sound which wafts and drifts around,
Excitement is crackling fireworks!
Crackling, crazy, cool!

Excitement is a bright orange flame burning like the sun,
Excitement is a bright red ball bouncing up and down
Great, good, gorgeous.

Jasmine S Ellis Rance (7)
Fairfield Park Lower School, Stotfold

Grounded

I'm grounded.
Typical. Right
I didn't even do it.
It was my little brother Max.
He broke the vase,
Smashed the glass,
Then dumped it all on me!
Or my seventeen-year-old sister Judy.
She killed the cat,
Bought a bat,
Then piled the trouble on me!
Or my twelve-year-old brother Sam.
He broke the bed,
Spilt the paint which was red.
And said it was all my fault!
I'm dead!
And grounded!

Megan Whooley (10)
Fern Hill Primary School, Kingston upon Thames

Snow Day

I woke suddenly
Something was wrong
An orange glow
Listen - nothing
No cars, no planes, no voices
Silence

Look out the window
Whooow - fantastic, stupendous, joy
Glistening white candyfloss
Listen - nothing
No garden, no path, no footprints
Just dazzling white silence

Crunching beneath boots
Unfamiliar knobbly shapes
Ice-covered leaves
Listen - nothing
No birds, no people, no trail
Crunch, drip, then silence

Tobogganing, snowmen, snowballs
Excited, *run!* Ice down the collar
Bright woolly hats, mittens, scarves
Listen, laughing, shrieking, shouting, barking
Children, parents, dogs
All the silence - *gone!*

Isabelle Rahim (9)
Fern Hill Primary School, Kingston upon Thames

Silence

Silence is a cave with no echo.
If you feel silence terror is upon you.
Silence . . .

Cassian McNicol (8)
Fern Hill Primary School, Kingston upon Thames

The Beast

It runs so fast towards you,
Then crashes down angrily.
It breaks into a million pieces,
Then retreats again.

It can be kind and gentle,
It sways from side to side,
And up and down.
It will feel cold against your skin,
But satisfyingly refreshing in the summer.

It lived before mankind,
And will live long after.
It offers life,
Yet steals life away too.

If it is destroyed,
We will have no hope of living.
It appears blue, green and many other colours too.
It's strong, yet fragile,
Threatening, but beautiful.

This wonderful yet dangerous beast,
The sea.

Nadia Sabania (10)
Fern Hill Primary School, Kingston upon Thames

Terror

Terror is when you're running from a zombie.
Terror is walking through a haunted house at night.
Terror is walking through a graveyard in the middle of the night.
Terror is having an operation, not knowing what is going to happen.
Terror is going to the dentist and having a needle in your mouth.
Terror is not knowing when you are going to die.

Dre Austin (9)
Fern Hill Primary School, Kingston upon Thames

Happiness

Happiness tastes like cotton candy.
Because if I buy cotton candy or something like it,
It gives me happiness.

Happiness looks like lots of PE subjects.
Because I like PE subjects and if I play lots of PE subjects,
It makes me happy.

Happiness smells like a new football or basketball.
Because I can smell new footballs or basketballs
And new footballs or basketballs smell good and make me happy.

If I touch happiness, I think it feels really soft.
Because soft is my best feeling,
And soft and cosy makes me happy.

And . . .
If I hear happiness
I think it would sound like my mum saying,
'I will buy you a brand new mp3!'
Because I want to buy a brand new mp3 or something,
I like these things, and they make me happy.

Wuseok Jung (9)
Fern Hill Primary School, Kingston upon Thames

Fire

Fire, it can take and destroy
Hopes and dreams
But if it went out
Would Earth be pulled apart at the seams?

Fire's our light, our life, our holy destruction,
We were born from flames and so shall we die.
Like a phoenix we are born but we are taken back to Earth
Back to water, back to fire, back to sky.

Gabriel Downer (10)
Fern Hill Primary School, Kingston upon Thames

About The Sea

The sea is full of creatures, the sea is full of seaweed,
The sea is full of wonderful things creeping up to me.
I was getting scared, just right there,
With no one else there but me.
I saw a shark fin, that made me blink in wonder,
Whilst it was coming right up to me.
It was swimming underneath my boat,
That made me frightened the most.
When I heard something make a noise,
I saw some more come towards,
Where an alarm warned me that it was a dolphin noise.
My heart stopped beating like a racing car,
Because I was relieved it was a bunch of dolphins.
Such beautiful creatures that I saw before me,
Twisting, spinning and jumping in and out of the sea.
I couldn't help but wonder what they were all thinking about.
Whilst I was sailing into the sunset they would not stop following me.
When I arrived on land they were all sad that I was going,
But were happy that I did not get eaten alive by sharks!

Abbie Hutchings (10)
Fern Hill Primary School, Kingston upon Thames

My Secrets

I am a Time Lord, I never grow up
I watched the dinosaurs become extinct
I am a volcano, as I kill hundreds
I watched the children of India die from illness
I am the lion who hunts down his prey
I heard a pin hit the ground
I found a pin in a haystack
I watched the Pink Panther being stolen
I am not who you think I am.

Abigail Bradley (9)
Fern Hill Primary School, Kingston upon Thames

I Am A Cheetah

Leopards on the ground,
Panthers in a tree,
They are very close to being like me,

For I am a cheetah
As fast as can be
But they could never catch me.

I hid around the bushes
Looking for something to eat,
I found a stripy zebra and sank in my sharp teeth,

The blood squirted everywhere,
My friends smelt it in the air.
They came and joined me
They pushed me out the way,
I went away
And will try again another day.

Rona Kamand (10)
Fern Hill Primary School, Kingston upon Thames

What Is Happiness?

The feeling of happiness is in touching,
It's fun and joyful
The fun is in happiness,
It's smiling, it's not just fun,
Like playing with your friends
But when it's your birthday you're really happy
And then you get presents,
From your friends and your family
Now you should be happy
Because you've got presents,
And the best thing is you're one year older!
That's what happiness is.

Mete Canli (8)
Fern Hill Primary School, Kingston upon Thames

The Senses

Once in the River Nile,
I met a crocodile
And it asked me
What could I see?
I said I saw sparkling water.
Which was also very clear,
Then it thoughtfully asked me,
What could I hear?
I said I heard waves,
Splashing about I could tell,
Then it asked me
What could I smell?
I said I smelt bad breath,
Coming from my lap,
Then it was too late,
Because the crocodile's jaws closed with a snap.

Dylan Marodeen (10)
Fern Hill Primary School, Kingston upon Thames

Family

Some families are good,
Some families are bad,
Some families are happy,
Some families are sad.

If there's a mixture of the two,
You'll be happy through and through.

Whatever happens,
Stick together,
And we'll be smiling whatever the weather.

Love your friends and family too,
Don't be surprised if they love you.

Zoe Robertson-Tingle (9)
Fern Hill Primary School, Kingston upon Thames

B!

B to me
Is the
Worst letter possi*le.
2nd to A
Means you're not that good.
Also the 1st letter of my
*rother's name,
Causes a whole load of
Trou*le too!
Always means you're 2nd
I think that * should *e
*anned!
*ees fly to us, then sting us,
Oooooowwwwwww!
I ask you now, what's the
Point of 'Bs'?

Harriet Warne (10)
Fern Hill Primary School, Kingston upon Thames

Fun

It tastes like the core
In a beautiful rainbow.
It smells of the sugar
On a colourful sweet.
It looks like the colour
On a gigantic firework.
It sounds like the laugh
Of a happy alien.
The colour is like the dye
On a silver sweet.
It feels like the texture
On flat aluminium.

Daniel Sykes (9)
Fern Hill Primary School, Kingston upon Thames

Terror At The Dentist

In the darkest corners of the Earth
In everything I said it was there
I knew I couldn't hide for long, it was after me
I felt me shiver, I knew it was all over
Why did the world have to end today,
Why not tomorrow?
I heard my name being called
I had to move but it was too late
I crept through the white doors,
Sat down,
Tasting the disgusting liquid poured in my mouth
Smelt the salty sweat on my face and . . .
Seeing the end of time . . .
Open your mouth and say, 'Argh!'
That's why I hate going to the dentist.

Emily Lucas (9)
Fern Hill Primary School, Kingston upon Thames

Sadness

Sadness is pain, fiery and hurtful,
It tries to blind,
It's full of tears and fire.

It's sinking and heartbreaking,
As a heart sinks into your throat,
You whimper, you cry and you hope.

Nothing is worse than sadness,
It's worse than having a five-inch cut,
It's cold, it's painful and deep.

You shout, you scream and you weep,
Sadness is bad, it will wake you from your sleep,
It's as hard as a rock and stiff.

Molly Morris (9)
Fern Hill Primary School, Kingston upon Thames

Every Feeling Has A Colour

Happiness is the colour of sunlight shining down on the dazzled
Earth,
Sadness is the colour of tears rolling down your cheeks
And making a puddle on the floor,
Rage is the colour of fire burning down a house
Right in front of you,
Excitement is the colour of your presents on Christmas Day
Waiting to be unwrapped,
Tiredness is the colour of your pillow waiting for you
To rest your sleepy head,
Nervousness is the colour of your clock with its hands ticking
As you wait for something to happen,
All these feelings make you, you
Who always feels different and has lots of feelings
Just like a rainbow has lots of colours.

Olivia Fox (10)
Fern Hill Primary School, Kingston upon Thames

My Hamster

My hamster is the cutest,
With his soft snowy fur.
He loves to eat his crunchy carrots,
That we give him through the bars,
Or he'll greedily scoff the little nuts
Into his big wide mouth.
But when I am fast asleep, he is wide awake,
And he runs and runs on his wheel
Like he's preparing for a marathon.
I love him so much, I think he likes me too.
He has funny, long, wiry whiskers
And a twitchy, pink little nose.
My hamster is the cutest.

Emma McCorquodale (10)
Fern Hill Primary School, Kingston upon Thames

The Amazing Creature

There is this creature,
Three legs are its main feature,
Its colour is very bright,
So it's difficult for him to hide at night,
His saliva is like glue,
Which makes it hard to chew,
The creature has a pointy nose,
As long as a hose,
And his ears,
The big spheres,
Are the cause of many fears,
But this creature is sad,
And will never be glad.

Arjun Bhushan (10)
Fern Hill Primary School, Kingston upon Thames

The Land Of Shroom

Oh have you ever heard of the land of Shroom,
Which is halfway between here and the moon?
It's a land of wacky, it's a land of weird,
There's a 4-headed monster with a bushy blue beard.
Every person has a teapot on their head,
And the whole of Shroom smells of fresh chocolate bread.
Oh have you ever seen all the bizarre creatures?
Especially the ones with the most peculiar features.
In the land of Shroom you can catch multi-fever,
What, you haven't heard of that? Well, me neither!
So now you have heard of the land of Shroom
It's a very strange place,
Halfway between here and the moon.

Jade Stewart (10)
Fern Hill Primary School, Kingston upon Thames

Terror In The Cellar

Creepy noises are all I can hear,
When they get louder it brings a tear,
The rats scatter everywhere.
Swishing wind around me,
It feels cold and deathly.
I cough and I splutter, I mutter
This smell is unbelievable of rotten food,
The walls look horrid, black and pale grey
It stiffens me head to toe.
It has hairy spiders' webs and smashed windows and mucky all around.
It smells of rotten fish and dirty books,
As well as abandoned monuments.

Max Haughton (9)
Fern Hill Primary School, Kingston upon Thames

Terror

Terror looks like a burning heart, killing and stopping peace
Like turning dreams and hope to death and painful fear.
Smelling like a dusty demon.
Ripping the poor lives out of defenceless people.
Will this ever stop?
People could die in a drop of deadly killing noises
And signs of death.
It will feel like losing all hope.
Killing everyone.
Making tastes like burning smoke.
It will feel like death.
It will be pitch-black.
Looking like deadly power fading all of hope.

Roozbeh Ashrafi (9)
Fern Hill Primary School, Kingston upon Thames

Hamsters

We bought a pair of hamsters
And named them Pip and Squeak.
They love to play together
And stuff their furry cheeks.

The wheel run makes them happy,
The fighting makes them mad,
The daytime makes them sleepy,
The noise wakes up my dad.

I love their funny faces
And how they twitch their nose.
But cleaning their dirty cage
Is gross, I suppose!

Ella Valentine (10)
Fern Hill Primary School, Kingston upon Thames

Sadness

It tastes like you bought an ice cream,
Which is very expensive
But then you find that it is really mouldy.
It sounds like a baby crying
Through an almost perfect movie.
It is a black room full of angry ghosts
And they're shouting at you.
It smells like smelly socks
That have been worn by a skunk.
It feels like touching an orange
That had been waiting for you for 15 years.
Sadness!

Alex Jacob (9)
Fern Hill Primary School, Kingston upon Thames

My First Goal

My first goal
Was a joyful moment
Crowds cheering madly
The opponents' manager shouting at the ref
Our players lifting me up
The opponents lying on the floor
The ball lying still in the back of the net
The referee telling players
'Come on, we need to take the corner'
The walking off, the keeper in tears
The screeching of the full time whistle
With me holding the trophy.

Henry Burns-Pegler (9)
Fern Hill Primary School, Kingston upon Thames

Summer

S ummer is when the sun shines brightly.
U nder shady trees we have our picnic.
N ights get shorter, day drifts on, the sun gets hotter.

H ot and sweaty are the long afternoons.
O n comes the sun cream when the temperature is 35^0
T he barbie sits on the decking while the ribs sizzle.

L ollies in the freezer for when we say 'please'.
O ut on our bikes for a summer's ride.
L ate hours until the sun goes out so I read until 9.
L azy nod-offs on the sofa as the clock strikes 3.
Y ou love it when the sun is out and you lick a lolly.

Ferney Usher (10)
Fern Hill Primary School, Kingston upon Thames

Courage

Courage smells like a man wishing to win his quest
An important one that can make his life change.
Courage feels like a point of the sharpest sword of a Roman soldier.
Courage looks like the boy in the distance
Fighting a dragon next to the most fearsome volcano yet to come
Courage smells like the sweat under King Henry VIII's armpits
Where spiders now crawl.
Courage's colour is orange, like birds' mythical blood.
Courage sounds like a bullet that goes through a heart
But not just any heart, a fairy tale heart.
Courage tastes like the liver of a human being just transplanted.

Filip Blazevic (9)
Fern Hill Primary School, Kingston upon Thames

The Life Poem

Life is golden, it is why we are still standing alive.
Life sounds like everything happy in the universe.
Life feels like the purest drop of water from the ocean
And a bar of gold combined.
Life makes everyone, spread with joy
It is the only thing that you need to survive.
Life tastes like the food that you will get
In a Michelin star restaurant.
Life smells like the purest food served delicately on a plate.
Life looks like everyone cheering one another
And people with good or bad property who still have a life.

Bigan Darvishy (10)
Fern Hill Primary School, Kingston upon Thames

Courage

Those who have fallen, will rise again
It's something so steady
That keeps you going through the pain,
Courage will last for a lifetime.

Courage is my friend,
Courage will keep you,
Laughing and standing up tall,
For while you believe,
Courage is for strength,
Your courage will cushion you forever!

Sinthuya Jayakumar (9)
Fern Hill Primary School, Kingston upon Thames

The Delivery

I went up to my run up,
Then I turned to face the enemy.
I came steaming in, charged right up to the wicket
And let The deep red, shining ball fly.
The ball zipped like a bullet towards the quivering batsman.
The bright cherry bounced sequin dust around the batsman's feet.
The ball clattered into the stumps
Sending the team and me crazy!
Then the bails dropped right into my open hands.
Out!

Archie Talman (9)
Fern Hill Primary School, Kingston upon Thames

Happiness

Happiness is bright colours, like yellow, orange and pink,
Bright colours are thoughts of happy things
It tastes very sweet
As sweet as pie
Soothing in your mouth and running down your throat
Sweet as a cherry from the sweetest cherry tree
Even sweeter than me
It feels very soft, like a pillow made from the biggest bear
From the darkest forest in the night cave
It sounds like a laughing crowd in a circus.

Junior Williams (8)
Fern Hill Primary School, Kingston upon Thames

To Mum

Why do I have to do my homework?
Why can't I go on the computer anymore?
Why do I have to write my thank you letters?
Why can't I jump on the floor?
Why Mum why do you interrupt me in my lair?
I ask you all this and what do you say?
You say:
Life isn't fair!

Well it isn't!

Lucy Honan (10)
Fern Hill Primary School, Kingston upon Thames

Surprise

Surprise is a present wrapped in green and blue
Please can you tell me, oh please do!
Surprise is a birthday cake with a creamy sponge
I am glad it is not covered in gunge!
Surprise is a brand new pet
And there's nothing better you can get!
Surprise is a beautiful bike gleaming red in the sun
What could be better?
Maybe a brand new chum.

Ruby Plunkett (8)
Fern Hill Primary School, Kingston upon Thames

My Idea Of Australia

A mazing Aborigines,
U nbelievable Uluru,
S unny skies,
T errific towns,
R owdy roos,
A dmirable art,
L ovely landscape,
I mpressive island,
A wesome Australia!

Jamie Thomson (9)
Fern Hill Primary School, Kingston upon Thames

Happiness

Happiness is everywhere
Happiness is now
Happiness is down the stairs
Happiness is wow!

Layla Shafquat (8)
Fern Hill Primary School, Kingston upon Thames

Tiger Cubs

Tiger cubs smell like long, dry grass.
Tiger cubs sound like squeaky cries.
Tiger cubs' colour looks like stripy, fluffy fur.
Tiger cubs remind me of newborn babies.
Tiger cubs feel like fluffy, soft cubs.
Tiger cubs start to drink from their mums.
The cubs learn from their parents.
They cuddle and snuggle and keep safe and warm.
Until they are old enough to run on their own.

Claire Harrison (10)
Fern Hill Primary School, Kingston upon Thames

The Groundsman

The groundsman is always moody,
Although I think he has a point,
The grass he cuts is smooth to the touch,
He paints the line of the crease as if it's a masterpiece.
The pitch is his pride and joy.
But when the team mess up the pitch
He shakes his arms in fury.
Altogether he is not so bad
Grumpy old Mr McLury!

Harry Vincent (9)
Fern Hill Primary School, Kingston upon Thames

Anger

It looks like fire, but it is anger.
It smells like boiling water, but it is anger.
It feels like lava, but it is anger.
It tastes like rotten cabbage, but it is anger.

Imran Ehab Malhan (9)
Fern Hill Primary School, Kingston upon Thames

Surprise

Surprise is a feeling of joy,
Like a present being given to you.
Surprise is like a Christmas present
That has been wrapped with sparkling gold and silver wrapping
paper.
Surprise is a birthday cake made especially for you,
With candles and chocolate icing too.
Surprise is when you see something new
Like an excited puppy who just loves you.

Jemi Sparks (9)
Fern Hill Primary School, Kingston upon Thames

Wonder

I wonder why clouds are white,
I wonder why skies are blue,
I wonder why we learn maths,
And the answer to 50x2.

I wonder why the world's round,
I wonder how to stand on my head,
I wonder why trees must lose their leaves,
I wonder why I've got to go to bed.

Marina McCready (9)
Fern Hill Primary School, Kingston upon Thames

Sadness

Sadness is a cold breeze blowing all the happiness away
And replacing it with a cold chill right down the spine.
Sadness is a thick box that you can't get out of.
Sadness is a drop of water dripping off your chin.
Sadness . . . is everywhere.

Jonathan Parker (9)
Fern Hill Primary School, Kingston upon Thames

Cycle, Cycle, Cycle

I was cycling down a steep hill.
I fell off my bike, I had to fix it.
I was in pain, covered in blood,
My bike was muddy just like soil.
I tasted my blood, it tasted like my mum's cooking.
All I could smell was my blood soaking down.
I thought I was done for, I thought I was dead.
But now it is time, time to say goodbye.

Gary Pitman (9)
Fern Hill Primary School, Kingston upon Thames

Pain

Pain is when you have an injection.
Pain is when you fall from the top of a building.
Pain is when someone pokes you with a very sharp knife.
Pain is when you trip over and fall on the hard ground.
Pain is when you bang your head on the wall.
Pain is when a ball hits your eye.
Pain is when your legs get stuck in the door.
So watch out, pain is everywhere.

Nabeel Shahpurwala (8)
Fern Hill Primary School, Kingston upon Thames

Terror

Terror lies at the mouth of a dragon's cave
It tastes hard and stale
Its colour is jet-black
It feels like intense pressure is squeezing you into nothingness
It smells of dark, wet, miserable days
It looks like a cold, empty face.

Euan Tasker-MacLeod (9)
Fern Hill Primary School, Kingston upon Thames

Anger

It smells like burnt toast or bin juice.
It is red, the colour of blood
And black, the colour of darkness.
It sounds like someone crying or screaming.
It tastes like lava or rotten cabbage
It looks like someone dead or being hanged.
It feels like boiling water.
It is anger!

Henry Samuels (8)
Fern Hill Primary School, Kingston upon Thames

Wonder

Wonder's like 'Alice in Wonderland'
Wonder why I am small?
Wonder why the world is tall
And the rest of it's all small?
Wonder why there's bark on trees?
Wonder why I have to say please?
Wonder why Tigger jumps high
And why can't I?

Zach Plunkett (9)
Fern Hill Primary School, Kingston upon Thames

Fear

Fear is the colour of darkness
It smells like rotten meat,
It tastes like the blood of a dead old man,
The horror inside me,
The confusion swirling inside my head,
Now total blackness.

Kitty Zhu (9)
Fern Hill Primary School, Kingston upon Thames

Light

The stars twinkle in the sky at night.
So does the moon which can shine very bright,
Like some kind of magic light.
As the sky becomes lighter
The sun will start to shine brighter
And the sky is clear.
Daytime is here, the children clap
Because daytime is here.

Tilley Brazil (10)
Fern Hill Primary School, Kingston upon Thames

Boil The Anger

The heat, like biting a hot chilli,
Anger, like angry rhinos' horns trying to hurt me.
The angriness takes the food and throws it on the floor,
Nobody sees it anymore,
I'm really angry
I need some running shoes,
So I can escape.

Sam Viney (9)
Fern Hill Primary School, Kingston upon Thames

Sailing

S ails flap in and out with the current of the wind,
A jib pulled tightly to make the boat fight the water,
I nky night sky hovered above my boat,
L ong ropes coiled around the mast,
I n the water, dolphins splashed happily,
N ever-ending sea stretched out before the boat,
G liding into the magic of my mind.

Charlie Allnutt (10)
Fern Hill Primary School, Kingston upon Thames

The Anger

As black as midnight skies.
It sounds as if there is thunder and lightning.
It looks like devils soaring through the sky.
It feels like fire burning in my hands.
It smells like fire burning in the distance.
It tastes like hot peppers.
I can't take this any longer.

Sacha Heaps (9)
Fern Hill Primary School, Kingston upon Thames

Terror

Terror tastes as dry as crackers diving down your throat,
Terror is in the air when people scream,
Terror is the colour of blood on a battlefield,
Terror smells as bitter as coffee,
Terror feels as dry as the outback on a hot summer's day,
Terror looks like a burning fire burning down black wood,
And terror never makes an error.

George Pepper (9)
Fern Hill Primary School, Kingston upon Thames

Silence

Silence is when you can hear a pin drop.
Silence is when you can hear a mouse squeak from its hole.
When you can only hear wind whistle through the leaves
That crash down to the ground.
Silence lays in an empty home when no one's there.
Silence,
No one can hear you!

Eyra Hughes (9)
Fern Hill Primary School, Kingston upon Thames

Forest And Me

I hear joy through the wind
When the birds are singing
I'm going in a cave with my friend Dave
It's very cold and I'm getting old
I'm climbing a tree with my teddy De
This is the end of Dave and me.

James Beazley-Long (8)
Fern Hill Primary School, Kingston upon Thames

All The Books I Have Read

All the books I have read
Sadly they're all the ones Mum said!
My third book I have read
It wasn't that much, only about beds.
The second book I never seemed to read?
Oh yeah, it was about teachers' needs.

Kieran Hanly-Green (9)
Fern Hill Primary School, Kingston upon Thames

Happiness

Happiness is like a baby laughing,
It smells like lilies flowering.
It feels like the softest feather, brushing against your skin,
Happiness tastes like a delicious, ripe and juicy peach.
Its colour is yellow, same as the beaming sun.
Happiness, sounding like tinkling bells.

Beverley Amanda Luu (9)
Fern Hill Primary School, Kingston upon Thames

Terror In My Veins

I saunter up the stairs.
I hear the sound of dry blood melting through the floorboards.
The stench of rotten apples wafts into my nose.
I feel petrified,
Anxiety courses through my veins,
I don't know where I will end up.

Sami Shori (9)
Fern Hill Primary School, Kingston upon Thames

Wonder

I wonder when I will smell?
I wonder when I will colour?
Wonder in the classroom?
Wonder why I don't walk?
I wonder why I am in wonderland?
I wonder why I am sleepy?

Dalia Aly (9)
Fern Hill Primary School, Kingston upon Thames

Love

Love tastes like the sweet cherry of the light tree
Love looks like the wonders of a rainbow.
Love feels like the warmest cuddle of the softest pillow.
Love is the colour of the brightest heart on Earth,
I think love smells like cocoa beans from the tropical cocoa tree.

Siobhan Flores Lynch (9)
Fern Hill Primary School, Kingston upon Thames

The Toy Boy

There was once a boy
Who acted like a toy
Never moving at all
He would sit there all day staring away
Acting just like a toy.

Sammy Sparks (10)
Fern Hill Primary School, Kingston upon Thames

Anger

Anger rushes through my veins
As black as the night sky,
My mother has abandoned me
Someone please tell me why.

I've lived with anger all my life
It's as bitter as bitter coffee,
I never seem to depart from it
And it never departs from me.

Anger grows inside me
It smells like burning coal,
It will stay inside for all my life
It destroys my heart and soul.

Since anger has lived with me
I will never forget,
How I treated it just like my own
My friend, love and pet.

Eden Igwe (9)
Fern Hill Primary School, Kingston upon Thames#

The Night

Swiftly sweeping up the remnants of the day,
Clear blue skies and cotton wool clouds,
Seemly glaring, swirling and swooping,
Lazily lurking whilst gracefully gliding,
Gloomily twisting and moodily twirling,
Vagrant, glittering, silky stars,
And a milky moon, guardian of the dark, mark of the night.

Ghostly trees swoosh and swish in the frozen breeze
As it creeps in,
Treacherous owls hoot in the silent, deadly distance,
Their eyes like the diamonds of terror and death -
Black and hypnotic,
Bats flapping whilst the crickets croak,
And fireflies dazzling and twinkling in the midnight melody,
Mystical and lonely,
Like a soft symphony swelling over the black destitute sky.

Sizzling stars scatter, vagrant in vast space,
A perfume packed with scents of towering mountains,
Golden, fiery sunsets,
And crystal fresh, icy waters.

A pearly harp of gloomy harmony,
A sullen flower blooming, across the wondrous world,
Exquisite, exuberant embroidery on the shawl of life,
A sapphire jewel on the necklace of creation,
Is the night.

Lavanya Sinha (10)
Highover JMI School, Hitchin

Terror Is Black

T error is black, as black as the night
E verywhere he goes he creeps and throws a pie
R otten eggs is a stench that he lets off
R otten fish is his taste to make you sick
O dd ghostly wind he sends through you
R eminding you of me.

I f he possesses you, you will die
S tirring you from sleep with nightmares.

B ehind you he creeps up scaring you
L ike a kid playing it with you
A playground
C ursing you, moawr ha, ha, ha
K nuckling you with fear . . .

I save you

A nd vaporise you
M oawr ha, ha, ha

I will strike
T onight blood spills.

James William Cullen Reed (10)
Highover JMI School, Hitchin

The River's Story

When I was happy
Mallards dabbling excitedly,
Dippers dipping relentlessly,
Minnows dodging the dippers,
But now I have rusty trolleys,
Slimy motor oil,
Beer cans,
Crisp packets in me!

Callum Defraine (11)
Highover JMI School, Hitchin

43

The Sea

The sea is like a busy road that churns and turns all the time,
With coloured fish like exuberant rainbows,
Covered in glitter, shimmering and shining
Through the aquamarine sea,
They chirpily swim around day and night
Like lightning striking a branch,
Sharks, clownfish, squid, octopus, whales, dolphins,
Lazy sea lions, electric eels, crawling crabs
Sticky starfish and sharp swordfish.
Always splish, splashing around in the deep blue sea.

Giant whales formidably take over the sea,
Bossing the town of fishes around,
Electric eels are the bright light of the night
Where it's dark and cold they shine,
Dolphins are the animals that caper elegantly across the waves,
Sharks are the beasts of the sea
That sadly scare other fish from the town,
The sea is like a busy road that churns and turns all the time.

Sofia Oliver-Rocha (11)
Highover JMI School, Hitchin

Sea

A dolphin swirling like a busy bee,
In the glistening blue sea,
Teal, turquoise, navy blues,
The crashing waves bringing good news,
Dolphins swimming swiftly around happily, like a cheerful hamster,
Seals squeaking, making the sea sound louder,
Starfish glowing in the deep blue sea,
Making the swirling, glistening turquoise,
Crashing, happy, loud, glowing sea looks shinier.

Alisha Malik (10)
Highover JMI School, Hitchin

Terror

Terror is a gigantic gust of wind
Passing through your body.
It makes you shake and shiver under the swarthy night sky
As it possesses your body.
Terror reminds you of a girl screaming for life
But no one can hear her.
She keeps running, screaming and crying
Like a siren until death kills her.
With the speed of light, it swoops behind you.
Then, it lurks in front of you with its silent footsteps.
Bang and you're gone!

It sounds like a roaring, crackling fire burning the world.
Soon it will spread through the universe,
Burning every creature in its path.
It smells like the suffocating smoke
Spreading through the city like a blackout.
Terror always wins.

Thanushan Aravinthan (11)
Highover JMI School, Hitchin

Happiness

It sounds like wedding bells on a sunny spring morning.
It tastes like luxurious chocolate oozing in your mouth,
It feels like a soft, warm, fluffy teddy bear.
It looks like a glamorous, sparkling diamond,
It smells like your new fruity perfume.

It sounds like children merrily laughing.
It tastes like rapturous raspberries dancing on your tongue,
It feels like a silky velvet blanket.
It looks like a carpet of bluebells,
It smells like radiant roses.

Tazmin Alam (11)
Highover JMI School, Hitchin

Rivers In The Jungle

As the river rushes on,
Fast, powerful and very strong.
Swivelling and twisting the river meanders
Passing monkeys, giraffes, lions and pandas

As a bird swoops overhead,
Suddenly a gunshot and it drops down dead.
The hunter's presence is felt everywhere,
On the ground and in the air.

Little fish with many colours,
Swim in and out of the reedy shadows.
Careful not to be seen or heard,
And become the next meal of the fish-eating bird.

The river's journey nears its end,
It passes around its final bend.
The sea is heard and comes into view,
An epic journey starts anew.

Samuel Waterworth (11)
Highover JMI School, Hitchin

The Moon

The moon is like a football
With chunks taken out of it,
The moon is like a tennis ball
Without the fuzz,
The moon is like the Earth
Without any life,
The moon is like a grape
Without the skin,
The moon is like an eyeball
Without the pupil,
The moon is a mystery.

Rhys Adams (11)
Highover JMI School, Hitchin

Water

Water drips,
Water splashes,
Water rages and water lashes,
Water creeps,
Water sneaks,
Water attacks and seeks,
For its latest victim to eat.

Water flows from side to side,
It also gleams like a glossy slide,
Schools of colourful fish happily swim by,
They like taking the waves for a ride.

Water plops,
Water drops,
Water never seems to stop,
Water also skips and jumps,
Whilst every living creature ceases and says watch.

Dami Bolarinwa (11)
Highover JMI School, Hitchin

I Am River

I flow like a river of beautiful diamonds
I crash and smash against smooth rocks
I skydive down glistening waterfalls
I watch my dippers restlessly bob,
Trying to catch a juicy meal
I stare as my outstanding kingfishers
Dart in and out of me
I cry as my pike head off as my ambassadors
I am constantly happy because I am a river.

Jacob Bryder (10)
Highover JMI School, Hitchin

Tigger The Rabbit

T igger is a woolly, white and smoky rabbit,
I nky grey spots stand out,
G iant hind feet,
G reat sharp nails,
E verything he has I love,
R abbits are cuter than everything else.

T iggers' wooden hutch is a fabulous home,
H e endeavours to escape,
E veryone should know him.

R avenous for grass he gnaws at his door,
A very overactive rabbit,
B ig tough bones,
B ooming brave body,
I love him so much,
T he most joyful rabbit in the world.

Elliot Gillard (11)
Highover JMI School, Hitchin

My Mum

My mum is a red rose
Glistening in the sun's rays
My mum is a big butterfly
Ready to help the world.
My mum is a cheerful person
Always laughing about
My mum is a fairy trying to do more
My mum is a rainbow,
Always the brightest.

Kirsty McKelvie (11)
Highover JMI School, Hitchin

Road Story

Driving along a raggedy road
Animals reaching to my headlights
I saw dogs' eyes, they had a sparkle in the eyes
They looked as if they were going to fly
One jumped and died
And the others looked as if they wanted to cry.

The owner came out and started to cry
I saw him he said, 'Why?'
He cried like a waterfall so I said,
'Don't worry it was his time.'
'But why?' he said
'I don't know why,' I said
'Well I can't change time,' I said
'Yes well I guess you are right,' he said
'And it is not like it is the end of time,' I said.

Rhys Ladd (11)
Highover JMI School, Hitchin

My Sister

My sister is a shining star against the night sky,
She is a snarling lioness,
She is a cat purring, bringing happiness into the room,
She is a shiny box full of surprises,
My sister is a unique, precious gem.
My sister is a scarlet-red rose,
My sister is a hot chocolate on a snowy day.

I love my sister.

Athena Chew-Hanson (11)
Highover JMI School, Hitchin

Love

Love looks like a pumping heart in a married couple,
Love sounds like a bird song on a sunny spring morning,
Love feels like the soft shivering feathers on a newborn chick,
Love tastes like rosy pink Turkish Delight,
Love smells like roses after the pouring rain,
Love reminds me of a great day on a toasted beach,
Love is the colour of sparkling red.

Love looks like a river of blood,
Love sounds like an eagle squawking after its lunch,
Love tastes like milk chocolate melting in your mouth,
Love smells like fresh candy waiting to be crunched,
Love reminds me of people smelling lavender after the rain,
Love is the colour of diamonds shining in the sun,
Love reminds me of family times.

Michael Brien (10)
Highover JMI School, Hitchin

My Life

I splash, splatter and meander through meadows
I've seen the Stone Age, the Victorians and the Noughties,
Now I watch the human race build up year by year.

Whilst I was dozing underneath the still sparkling stars,
I was poisoned by monstrous factories
Vomiting their sick into me.
I'm full of crisp packets, beer bottles and trolleys
The humans eat me away like beasts
Which are rusting away beneath my murky skin.
I'm now dying but no one cares
When will I be revived?

Whilst resting in the healthy wild woods,
I gradually close my eyes forever.

Jake Oliver (11)
Highover JMI School, Hitchin

Joy

It sounds like lots of people screaming.
It is a colour of glistening disco lights.
It looks like an exciting game of football.
It feels like you are cheering someone up.
It reminds me of being at an exciting party
Dancing to the great music with my best friends.
You make it by being funny to other people.
Finally it smells like people blissfully eating sweet popcorn together.

Harry Minnis (10)
Highover JMI School, Hitchin

The River

The silky smooth river,
Sliding slowly down rocky waterfalls,
Colourful kingfishers perching
On the side of the riverbanks.
Moorhens bobbing, bubbles bursting
Minnows swimming, beavers building on the river.

Byron Stuart (11)
Highover JMI School, Hitchin

Be Careful

A tyrant lizard
Be attentive, attentive
It's got spikes
So don't go near

It's really colossal
And really strapping
So be really careful
And don't get sent to the past.

Kaushala Davidson (7)
Kingsbury Green Primary School, Kingsbury

The Time Named Death

Suddenly I heard the door *slam!*
Horrifyingly, I heard a gun, *bang!*

I stood with a bullet through my chest,
I felt the blood run though my vest.

The blood rushed to my head,
So I tried to shake my leg,
But I already knew my fate.

Seconds turned to minutes
As I lay . . .

I couldn't find the strength to say,
Because my breath was taken away,
I decided it was the time to pray . . .

Thank you, Lord, for this day,
May I RIP as I lay.

My sight blurred and full of sorrow,
I thought I would never see tomorrow.

I laid feeling blessed
As I closed my eyes for eternal rest.

Aaron Vowles (11)
Kingsbury Green Primary School, Kingsbury

Boring Journey

Stretching into the horizon
Headlights staring into the wet road
No moving
Nothing
Nothing
No games to play
Nothing to see.

Megan Long (10)
Kingsbury Green Primary School, Kingsbury

Winter

Winter, winter,
The lovely days,
I love it because
St Nick will be here.
Winter, winter,
Snow as white
As St Nick's beard.
Winter, winter,
As cold as a car,
So cold that you have to
Wrap up your car.
Winter, winter,
As cold as a barn.
Winter, winter,
As cold as a cold bell.
Winter, winter,
As white as a fish.
Winter, winter,
As cold as ice.

Huda Ali (7)
Kingsbury Green Primary School, Kingsbury

The Haunted House

The darkest night,
No one shall escape my sight
Or you will see my darkest fear.
On this dark, spooky night
You will get such a fright
As you near this spooky sight.
Don't bump into the giant light,
The frozen light,
Or you will turn to stone!

Samuel Mongare (7)
Kingsbury Green Primary School, Kingsbury

Famous Lights!

Lights flashing in my eyes
Flash!
Flash!
Flash!
Why can't they leave me alone?
Oh yeah! I'm famous, that's why,
Flash!
Flash!
Flash!
Oh man! Paparazzi again, please!
Leave me alone.
Flash!
Flash!
Flash!
I'm only a child!
Flash!
Flash!
Flash!
Please, give me peace for once!

Rochelle Hay (11)
Kingsbury Green Primary School, Kingsbury

My Sister

Happiness for me means
Sharing my whole life with you.
Happiness means seeing all
Our dreams come true . . .

Happiness for me means
Knowing the greatest gift in life -
The love that I have always found in you,
My wonderful newborn sister!

Mehwish Sohail (11)
Kingsbury Green Primary School, Kingsbury

The Haunted House

The wind was howling very loud,
Leaves were dancing all around.
I called for help but . . .
Nothing,
Nothing,
Nothing replied back.

The wind roared louder,
The taunting clouds came together,
Lightning streaked across the sky.
Looking for shelter I went into the house
Which loomed over me.

Cautiously I walked in,
Bats screeched, cats purred
And dust blew into my face.
I walked further into the house.
Suddenly I heard a shriek!
What could it have been . . . ?

Shanji Sritharan (11)
Kingsbury Green Primary School, Kingsbury

Nature

What can you see?
The sun glistening from the sky.

What can you see?
The birds flying from the north.

What can you see?
The navy blue ocean swimming through the river.

What can you see?
A group of butterflies dancing
In a sensational style.

Manahil Mehmood (8)
Kingsbury Green Primary School, Kingsbury

The Night Sky

At night I eat some apple pie
Just looking up in the sky.
I can see the gleam of the twinkling star
Looking down so I can feel so calm.

I can see the glow of the chalky moon,
It's just so cool!
I just want to buy a star-shaped kangaroo
That is polished with a nice chilly moon.

I can see the dark sky,
What can I do? It is so high
Making everybody die.
Oh my God, isn't that a big lie?
What can you see?

Nadiya Osman Faqi (8)
Kingsbury Green Primary School, Kingsbury

The Gang Life

Kids carry around names to gain fame,
Knives, guns, thinking it's a toddler's game,
But truly it's worthless pain.

These worthless victims of the media,
Those poor souls who've forgotten
How to dream the real life around here . . .

Mothers, fathers, uncles, aunts, brothers and sisters,
All worried and petrified,
Thinking whether they will live to the next day.

We need to wake up from this dream
And live reality
Because death is *guaranteed!*

Hodo Ali (11)
Kingsbury Green Primary School, Kingsbury

Chocolate

I am chocolate,
Everybody likes to eat me.
Chocolate is made out of milk,
I like Dairy Milk.

Chocolate is made out of dairy milk,
Not hairy milk.
Slim milk is dirty,
Dairy milk is tasty.

Chocolate is simple and yummy,
It reminds me of the colour brown.
Brown is the colour of chocolate.
Chocolate! Chocolate! Chocolate!

Sofia Remtula (8)
Kingsbury Green Primary School, Kingsbury

Outside The Doors

It is a lovely day,
It is time to go and play.
The sky is blue,
My balloon flew.

The trees have a wave
While a man lives in a cave.
In the evening the sky is pink,
As my sisters give me a wink.

The clouds are white,
The bees want to bite.
There is an aeroplane in the sky,
There is a bird flying high.

Monica Mootealoo (8)
Kingsbury Green Primary School, Kingsbury

Bullies

Don't be rude
Don't be snappy
Don't be cruel
Don't steal
Or you'll be in trouble
It won't be my fault
It won't be the teacher's
It won't be your friends'
It will be yours
Don't be a bully
Be kind 'cause you're
Like everyone else.

Taja Coombes (10)
Kingsbury Green Primary School, Kingsbury

The Beach

Strolling on the beach
The sand cool and soothing the soles of my feet
Crabs scuttling by the sea
The whales singing in the calm waves.
Laying down, staring at the cloudless sky
Slowly drifting away into my own wonderland
Where flowers spin like dancing angels,
The seagulls like singing aeroplanes fly.
Waking up by a trickle of water, walking back home
I pick up a soft but hard seashell,
Put it to my ear, hear the sound of soft waves.
When the day is finally over, tears eventually fall . . .

Chyna Buena, Daniel Mbo & Rochelle Hay (11)
Kingsbury Green Primary School, Kingsbury

A Dazzling Day

As the blazing sun rises in the distance
Droplets of perspiration slowly fall
Down my smooth, silky face.
Summer has finally arrived!

On this glorious summer day
I play on the golden, glistening beach
Till dusk.

But I wish I could play forever . . .
And ever . . .
And ever . . .
And ever.

Rufa'a Masoud (10)
Kingsbury Green Primary School, Kingsbury

Sandy Beach

On the sandy beach where people reach
And the children all play around.

On the rippling beach where the crabs can reach
And the crabs go scuttle, scuttle.

On the calming beach where no people reach
It's silent *shh! shh! shh!*

On the fading beach where the seagulls go flutter, flutter, flutter
And the people stand around.

On the cloudy beach where the children go to sleep
And the dolphins go nip, nip, nip.

Rachael Oluwaseyi Aina (8)
Kingsbury Green Primary School, Kingsbury

It Doesn't Matter!

It doesn't matter how people look
Because . . .
Sometimes they are skinny,
Sometimes they are mad,
Sometimes they are funny,
Sometimes they are sad,
Sometimes they are tiny,
Sometimes they are fat,
Sometimes they are bald
And sometimes they are flat,
But it doesn't matter.

Isabel Narayan (10)
Kingsbury Green Primary School, Kingsbury

The Death Of A London Youth

The sharp blade pierced through my skin and flesh
Leaving a scar that looked like it had been
Inflicted by something inhuman.
Barrow loads of crimson-red blood
Poured out of my system
Like water from a cup.
As I took my last breath,
A bright white light blinded my eyes,
Assuring that it was my final hour.
My soul arose from my body
And floated to the gateway of Heaven.

Kunmi D'angelo Ojo (11)
Kingsbury Green Primary School, Kingsbury

Summer Sun

S noozing people lively, awake
U nusual, bright colours are seen and worn
M agical happiness fill the individuals inside
M enace rarely happens
E gos are boldy shown
R aving children run wild in the space of the fields

S pewing heat flies into the calm atmosphere
U gly memories fade away
N atural things regularly happen.

Jada Eduvie (10)
Kingsbury Green Primary School, Kingsbury

On The Sandy Beach

On the sandy beach where
The seagulls all flutter and squeak.

On the sandy beach where
The waves don't reach and the crabs all hide and peek.

On the sandy beach where
The cats all screech
And the people all put on their hats.

Candice John-Baptiste (8)
Kingsbury Green Primary School, Kingsbury

Fantastic FIFA Football

Peter Crouch with a hard-headed goal, cheer!
Lionel Messi, the best player in the world.
Zlatan Ibrahimovic is the second best player, *crunch!*
Wayne Rooney got a broken leg, *ooooh!*
Fernando Torres is a Liverpool striker but he can score.
Arjen Robben lost to Inter Milan, *ooooh!*

Ayman Elmi (8)
Kingsbury Green Primary School, Kingsbury

Monster Rap

Look, there's a monster coming down the street,
It looks so tiny and it ain't that neat.
It's always mad, also bad,
It doesn't look like it's ever sad.

It lives over there in the dirty dump,
On the back of its head there is a bump.
It's full of trash and rotten mash,
Its best friend is a boy called Ash.

It has a taste for lots of cash,
The food it hates is rotten mash.
It don't look like it slurps and munches,
It looks like it burps and crunches.

All it does is hops and jumps,
Like a frog on speed bumps.
It really likes to run and scoot,
It fights like a big fat brute.

All its punches really hurt,
It goes round wearing a skirt.
Sometimes it wears a red shirt,
At king fu it punches dirt.

Miles Salt (9)
Langham Primary School, Colchester

Monster Rap

I am a monster, hairy and scary
I will always vary
And I have caught a fairy
And I love dairy.

I am a monster who lives in the sea
I come when you are with me.
He loves a good cup of tea
His house is under the sea and he uses a key.

He has four eyes like rainbows that are round
Did I mention he lives underground?
And he has a pet hound
That likes to play in the playground.

He has a thing for cash
With his terrible mash
He will give you a smash
He has a terrible rash.

Thomas James Harris (9)
Langham Primary School, Colchester

Monster Rap

I see a monster, big and fat,
He's hairy and spotty with a bump on his back.
He has brilliant big ears and a huge ugly nose,
Shining, sharp teeth and slimy green toes.

That monster eats horrible things, you know,
Like mice and rats and slugs and bats,
And little dead bees and squashed up peas
And snails and worms and things that squirm.

Isabel Dickie (8)
Langham Primary School, Colchester

Monster Rap

My monster lives in the grass
And never goes to class.
My monster has great big hands
And never understands.

My monster is very scary
And is very hairy.
My monster is very fat
And is as big as a cat.

My monster loves musical chairs
And has lots of toy bears.
My monster doesn't cheat
And always gets a seat.

He eats out of the bins
The leftovers in tins.
He walks around in a mood
Monsters think he is so rude.

Isaak Ord (9)
Langham Primary School, Colchester

Monster Rap

Here is the night stalker
He's a very good talker.
He's got a lot of legs
And he's got four heads.

He lives on Planet Ripper
He's an excellent knitter.
He tears up all his food
And he's very, very rude.

He munches and crunches
And eats lots of lunches.
He slurps with a straw
When it splats on the floor.

He's got an enormous brain
Nearly the size of a crane.
You mustn't make him mad
Or you will feel quite sad.

William Thompson (9)
Langham Primary School, Colchester

Monster Rap

My monster's big and hairy
My monster's ginormous and scary
My monster has wings like a fairy
My monster eats a lot of dairy

My monster slurps and burps
My monster flirts and hurts
And goes round wearing a skirt
My monster thinks he's an expert

My monster glides and collides
My monster loves the slides
And my monster flies

My monster eats guns and buns
My monster eats particular guns
My monster is as fat as a pig
My monster loves to dig, dig, dig.

Eli Smith (9)
Langham Primary School, Colchester

Monster Rap

The pink, spotty monster is very big
He is scruffy and wears a wig
Oh, the ugly monster is sat
And looks like a rat
He eats all day and that's my rap!

Ocean Green (7)
Langham Primary School, Colchester

I Am A Monster

I am a monster very scary
I am a monster very hairy
I am a monster who's loving ham
I am a monster riding a lamb
I am a monster eating lots
I am a monster cleaning pots
I am a monster who likes jam
I am a monster making a bang
I am a monster running fast
I am a monster driving a car
I am a monster that is big
I am a monster who's never mean
I am a monster drooling lots
I am a monster in the bath
I am a monster going to bed
I am a monster fast asleep.

Sam Finch (9)
Langham Primary School, Colchester

I Saw A Monster

I saw a monster, slim and small,
Looked like it was tiny but it was really quite tall.
I saw a monster with hands like a spade,
I saw my monster in a very long parade.
I saw a monster as loud as Class 3,
I saw a monster getting things free.
I had to say goodbye to my monster
And it said goodbye to me.

Abbie Wells (7)
Langham Primary School, Colchester

Monster Rap

Listen everyone, and you'll be in luck
Let me introduce my monster, Chuck
He's round and fat with a taste for hats
His favourite ones are baseball caps.

He's hairy, he's scary and a little lairy
But he dances and prances around like a fairy
He likes to catch bats for his lunch
Which he eats really loudly with a big loud *crunch!*

Chuck has wheels instead of feet
He rolls around, it's so neat
He lives in a hut made from sticks
And if his hut breaks it is hard to fix!

Frankie Beedon (9)
Langham Primary School, Colchester

Blob

Blob is a monster who sits in the loo
She lives in a house next to the zoo
She spits very far
Her favourite thing is strolling and rolling
She's as fat as a rat
And as round as a pound.

Blob is a monster who eats very messy
And likes to eat with her friend, Nessy
Blob is a monster who doesn't wear clothes
And she has big, fat, hairy toes.

This is Blob, fat not scary
But is very, very hairy.

Erica Mateer (9)
Langham Primary School, Colchester

Monster Rap

I am a monster called Eeyore
I am as thin as my lounge door
Dancing around like a fairy
Eating verbs from a dictionary

I think that I am a fluffy cat
When I'm wearing my shiny hat
I have thousands of smelly fleas
I also love eating car keys

I am as smelly as a nappy
I am always feeling happy
When I play by the rule
I also play it really cool.

Lily-Jade Bartholomew (9)
Langham Primary School, Colchester

Monster Rap

I know a monster whose name is Tilly
And she likes to act really silly.
She has lots of hair which is full of mud
And her favourite drink is a pint of blood.

She is big and loud and heard from all around,
Her laugh is such an amazing sound.
She eats like an enormous pig
And after she's eaten, she does a little jig.

Tilly stomps down the street
And plays with the kids, that's so sweet.
She likes to live in the drains,
But gets really wet when it rains.

Ella Palmer (9)
Langham Primary School, Colchester

My Imaginary Friends

The friends I've got
Live in a pot,
There's room for them all
'Cause they're tiny and small.
One is called Sid,
He operates the lid.
It will open and close,
So mind your nose.
If you're having a look,
Just read this book.

One girl is called Pam,
She lives with Sam.
They cook everyone ham,
It's all they ever eat
Because the honey glaze is so sweet.
The babies are in the shape of feet,
Their tiny hands have so much heat.

Maja Smith (9)
Merstham Primary School, Merstham

Spuddy

I have a really special buddy,
His name is Spuddy.
He hates going out in the rain,
When he pops my balloon he's a real pain.
He used to like it on my bed,
But now he can't because I've got a bunk bed.
He's not very tall
But oh boy, he can run fast for the ball,
But I still love my dog.

Henry Jablonski (9)
Merstham Primary School, Merstham

In My Garden

In my garden
I can see the dog next door
Lying in the shade
His tongue hanging on the floor
I wonder what he is thinking.

In my garden
I can see birds on the ground
Talking and eating bread
Pecking and pushing around
I wonder if they like each other.

In my garden
I can see a big blue slide
I play on it with my sister
We love playing outside
I wonder if it will be sunny tomorrow.

Leah Hutchings (9)
Merstham Primary School, Merstham

Animal House!

My cats, cute and lazy.
My rats, greedy and mad.
My dog is funny and crazy,
She likes to chase the ball.
My turtles, they are quite small.

My hamster, she stands on top of her wheel,
Then falls head first.
My fish, they like to swim and play in the bubbles.
My snails, they are a bit too slimy.
My cute guinea pigs, they like sleeping and eating.

My pets, sixteen in all.

Cody Wren (9)
Merstham Primary School, Merstham

Skiing

Went skiing today,
My first time ever on snow,
Zoomed down all the way.

Went skiing today,
Felt as free as an eagle,
Up the lift again.

Went skiing today,
The snow is starting to melt,
Mountains are icy.

No skiing today,
I've had a wonderful time,
The snow is all gone.

Adam Rayner (8)
Merstham Primary School, Merstham

Caterpillar

Caterpillar, caterpillar, long and furry,
In a hurry to get to Surrey,
Where the plants are green
And the grass is lush,
Where a ladybird waits
To make him blush.

Rebecca Bowman (8)
Merstham Primary School, Merstham

The Storm

The sea is blue,
The waves are rolling in fiercely,
The sky is dark.
The rain begins to fall down
And thunder roars.
The lightning strikes and
Lights up the sky and the sea.
Suddenly the storm is over
And the sea is calm again,
Gentle, rolling waves
Coming in to shore.

Sam Gardiner (9)
Merstham Primary School, Merstham

Mood Months

Jolly January
Fantastic February
Awkward April
Merry May
Joyful June
Jumpy July
Active August
Sunny September
Odd October
New November
Delightful December.

Robyn McCurry (8)
Merstham Primary School, Merstham

Vampire

My best friend is a vampire,
She always sleeps in school,
She never goes on sunny days,
She hardly goes in the pool.

When I go to her house
She always lets me lend,
I don't care what people say or think,
We are always the best of friends.

Jessica Ayres (9)
Merstham Primary School, Merstham

My Bike

I love to ride my bike everywhere,
In the park, really fast, with my friends,
Up and down the hills as fast as we can go,
Getting muddy and wet is great fun,
Racing and doing tricks we like to do.
I love riding my bike to school,
Riding my bike is lots of fun.

Christian Bright (9)
Merstham Primary School, Merstham

Fish

They swim past you quickly
And they are very prickly,
But then comes that mean 'thing',
With teeth as sharp as a knife
And a very horrible life!
The 'thing' tries to eat them
But misses and bites a rock,
It screams in agony
And it lands on a block.

The fish are now happy
And some of them are snappy.
Some fish are colourful
And others are just grey.
Some fish are evil
And some are cruel.

Some fish are as hard as a rock,
Others are just plain,
But all fish are different
And unique in their own ways.
Some fish are strange
And they are impossible to arrange.

Fish are clever,
Fish are colourful,
Fish are wicked
And they are very skilled.
Fish are cool and they don't drool,
Never underestimate the power of fish!

Thomas Bradbury (10)
Rokeby School, Kingston upon Thames

Fingers

When I woke up this morning and got out of bed,
I had a headache so I rubbed my head.
The touch was all squidgy, my hand went right through,
And I screamed so loud that the birds went cuckoo!
The family rushed in, they said, 'What's wrong, son?'
I said, 'It's my fingers and head; they're as soft as a bun!'
But I was wrong, it was much more than that,
When I touched my belly it just went splat!
But there was one good thing that was really great,
For all these reasons I was losing weight!
I started shrinking extremely fast,
It really felt like I was back in the past!
My family were watching, watching in awe,
Dad was so amazed that he dropped his saw!
It went bouncing along the table, just missing my leg,
Then it carried on going and it hit the peg!
I felt little and scared, I felt vulnerable and weak,
And I honestly thought I'd stay like this for a week!
Then my sister came in and she started to scream,
She was so amazed that she dropped her ice cream!
It landed on me, I was freezing to death,
I just about heard Dad mutter under his breath!
He ran down the stairs, picked up the phone too,
He rang the police, who came quite soon.
They went through the door and up the stairs,
But when they got there I'd vanished into thin air!
So I'll tell you now, when the touch is soft on your head,
Don't touch it again or else you'll be dead!

Gregory Hunt (10)
Rokeby School, Kingston upon Thames

The Secret Behind Doughnuts

Out of all the things I've seen in my life
I've never looked at this feisty life.

It has one eye in the middle
And many coats of delight,
I can't believe
I've never seen it in my life.

You can impress me with laughter,
But I'll look the other way,
And see this creamed softy,
Which will always find my way.

Now those of you who know me
Will know what I'm talking about,
You can get a six-pack special
Or a twelve-pack medal.

Now I like to go for a membership option,
That's decorating your own
And going crazy with your sugar adoption.

I guess it's time to tell you
What on earth I am going on about,
Because at the moment it sounds
Like I have a serious sugar rush.

So here it goes, after six verses,
The moment of justice.
It's doughnuts and sprinkles
And sugar and sweetness.

Alex Lewis Whitaker (10)
Rokeby School, Kingston upon Thames

77

The Magic Box
(Based on 'Magic Box' by Kit Wright)

I will put in my box . . .
The sound of the flapping wings of the bird,
The roaring from the mighty lion,
The nails of the man touching his lips.

I will put in my box . . .
The hitting of the thundering drums,
A taste of a juicy orange,
The soft sheep's wool.

I will put in my box . . .
The claws of a man,
The nails of a mighty lion,
A glimpse of the sunny sky.

I will put in my box . . .
The huge Godzilla destroying the buildings,
The two-headed creature,
The sword made out of the sunny sun.

I shall surf in my box on
The huge, fierce waves of the southern sea,
The beautiful orange blue beach,
The red, fluffy moon.

Jacopo McConnell (9)
Rokeby School, Kingston upon Thames

My Cat, Bonnie

Bonnie is as soft as a scarf,
Bonnie's eyes are as big as bulldozers,
Bonnie's ears are as sensitive as a satellite,
Bonnie is as naughty as naughty can be,
Bonnie's life is fun.

Thomas Busby (8)
Rokeby School, Kingston upon Thames

The Trenches

It was the coldest, darkest night of the year,
We felt the dampness chill our bones.
Our breath floated up like frozen fear
And nobody dared to think of home.

The sound of gunfire filled my head,
And the deafening roar of the falling shells
Made it hard to think of my friends lying dead,
The whining bombs were their funeral bells.

I could see the poppies on the trench's ledge,
And rows of boots churning up the mud.
Small brown rats scuttled over the edge,
The dead sergeant's coat was blotted with blood.

The acrid smells of the powder and smoke
Filled our nostrils like rotten waste.
The drifting gas made us gag and choke
And the ash gave our rations a bitter taste.

Frost covered our helmets, coats and hands,
Numb fingers round our weapons curled,
As snow began falling on no-man's-land,
The most desolate place in all the world.

Julius Dunfoy (10)
Rokeby School, Kingston upon Thames

Senses

S enses are messages to your brain
E ars send sound signals like the noise of a train
N oses send smells, good, bad and mixed
S enses, they're nature's magic tricks
E yes are like cameras in your head
S enses, like touch, feel good but shut down in bed.

Fergus Norgren (10)
Rokeby School, Kingston upon Thames

Magic Box
(Based on 'Magic Box' by Kit Wright)

I will put in my box . . .
The brightness of a red cloth,
The venom from the slippery snake,
The tough, tame tiger creeping through the grass.

I will put in my box . . .
The smell from the rotting flesh,
The blade of the assassin's knife,
The ear-splitting roar of the dragon.

I will put in my box . . .
A T-rex stomping through the jungle,
The Minotaur smeared with blood,
The blast from a gun.

My box's hinge is fashioned from the wood of a tree,
My box's sides are made of dragon scales,
My box's skin is fashioned from tiger skin.

I will swim in my box,
I will ride the waves,
I will watch the sunset in my box.

Joe Robertshaw (10)
Rokeby School, Kingston upon Thames

Happiness

Happiness is the colour orange,
Happiness is little children laughing and playing in the sand,
Happiness is little kids running in the park,
Happiness is like spicy BBQ chicken on lovely kebabs,
Happiness is like a squashy, brand new kitchen sponge,
Happiness is as soft as a lovely chocolate with melted chocolate
sauce.

Zachary Robbins (9)
Rokeby School, Kingston upon Thames

The Sensory Poem

The taste so sweet
So tangy in the mouth
An explosion of bitter but sweet taste
Its colour so bold
Once tasted, you can never stop eating it.

The sound so smooth
Like a violin
Like a piano
I love it.

The smell so strong
Like a field of flowers
Blowing in the summer wind
And the pollen protecting you.

The look so beautiful
Like a dancing fairy
Glowing in the night.

It feels so smooth
But still quite bumpy
The thing I love so much is *my family.*

Daniel Carr (10)
Rokeby School, Kingston upon Thames

Silence

Silence is invisible, like air
Silence is pure air, like the night sky
Silence is quiet, like no sound
Silence is sweet, like sugar paper
Silence is silent boys in exams
Silence is quiet on my ears
Silence reminds me of work, *no!*

William Martin (10)
Rokeby School, Kingston upon Thames

Winter

This season comes every year,
Winter is its name when it comes here.
The winter is cold and there is no sun,
Everyone is inside having fun.

Everyone's favourite day comes in this season,
Christmas lunch and presents are the reason.
Grandparents, aunties and uncles come
To join us for some party fun.

Great joy comes when snow falls,
So children can fight with snowballs.
Make a wall for your defence,
Make a hole for offence.

Building snowmen with your friends,
Hoping play will never end.
Building the snowman greater and greater,
Telling your mum, 'I'll be back later.'

Tom Usher (10)
Rokeby School, Kingston upon Thames

Winter

Winter's morn, all cold and bright,
The snow as white as a polar bear.
We make snow angels throughout the day
And for tea, biscuits and hot chocolate.
Winter's evening, Christmas is coming!
With crackers all to pull,
And feasts and laughter,
But most of all, happiness.
Winter's night, now we've gone to bed . . .
Ssshhh! Don't make a sound.

Vivek Haria (10)
Rokeby School, Kingston upon Thames

Snowflakes

The sky is as grey as a blazer,
It is coming,
It is falling like confetti from a newlywed,
It is coming,
It sways from side to side like a rocking chair,
It is coming,
It is softer than a baby's skin,
It is coming,
It is colder than ice cream,
It is coming,
It looks like diamonds,
It is coming,
It is as runny as honey,
It is coming,
Yet it's as hard as diamonds.
The snowflakes are coming,
The snowflakes are coming.

Buster Parr (10)
Rokeby School, Kingston upon Thames

My Penguin

My penguin likes fish and crabs,
My penguin's name is Kobra,
My penguin likes surfing,
My penguin is a very fast swimmer,
My penguin was born in 2003,
My penguin is stronger than two million sharks,
My penguin ate Jupiter whole!
My penguin swam across the Atlantic
And back in five seconds!
My penguin is an emperor!

Joshua Thompson (8)
Rokeby School, Kingston upon Thames

A Dragon

A puff of smoke behind that door
A blow of wind behind that door
A red flash behind that door
A burning sound behind that door
An ear-piercing scream behind that door

The door creaked open
A green scale behind that door
The door creaked further
A tail appeared behind that door

Then I realised suddenly
I shut the door instantly

I must tell you
I must tell you
A dragon!

Josh Agrawal (10)
Rokeby School, Kingston upon Thames

The Tiger

Inside the deluxe tiger's fur, the river of water,
Inside the river of water, the bloodstains,
Inside the bloodstains, the sandy desert,
Inside the sandy desert, the slimy tongue,
Inside the slimy tongue, the frozen river,
Inside the frozen river, the big, huge eyes,
Inside the big, huge eyes, the rabbit's fur,
Inside the rabbit's fur, the tiger's massive, sharp fangs,
Inside the tiger's massive, sharp fangs, the cold, soft snow,
Inside the cold, soft snow, the short, spiky hair,
Inside the short, spiky hair, the flexible green grass,
Inside the flexible green grass, the huge, rocky forest,
Inside the huge, rocky forest, the tiger's deluxe fur.

Rahul Joshi (9)
Rokeby School, Kingston upon Thames

The Dog

He wallows in the mud
And walks around on four legs

He is a fluffy ball with a tail
And he thinks it's normal

He buries his waste in the garden
And he thinks it's normal

He chases squirrels and birds
And he thinks it's normal

He smells like dirt and doesn't wear clothes
And he thinks it's normal

Well let me tell you something,
It is very normal.

Ian Hitch (10)
Rokeby School, Kingston upon Thames

Tom And Jerry

T om and Jerry are tortoises,
O ver their body is a hard shell.
M an-handled they do not like to be

A nd under their shell is a scaly body with scaly legs
   and a scaly tail
N ot big are they, but very slow, by the way
D own they live in the Mediterranean, but upright

J erry is the smallest of the two but is the fastest of the two
E very night they silently sleep and in the morning
   they take a peep and then go back to sleep
R ambling round the garden
R ushing to eat up the delicious food
Y um-yum, their favourite food is dandelions.

Oliver Khurshid (8)
Rokeby School, Kingston upon Thames

Sensory Poem

This creature,
It tastes like sour sweets
Burning in my mouth!

It looks like a small, fizzing bomb . . .
About to explode!

It smells like fresh coconuts hanging on a tree,
The smell is so refreshing and sweet.

It feels rather bumpy and rough,
Like a mountain with scaly rocks.

It sounds like a clock ticking
And it pops and gives a burst of
Sweetness and energy into my ears.

Thomas Oliver (10)
Rokeby School, Kingston upon Thames

What Am I?

I swim in the sea,
I have an extremely hard shell,
I am as slow as an ant,
I am really wise,
I have a shell on me,
I am kind and good at hiding,
I am related to the tortoise,
Seagulls drop me from cliffs to break my shell,
I can go into my shell,
I have a scaly body,
I am a reptile,
I have a short neck,
I have large eyes.

Brandon Chau (8)
Rokeby School, Kingston upon Thames

The Bunny

Inside the bunny's tooth, the hill of velvet,
Inside the hill of velvet, the bunny's ear,
Inside the bunny's ear, the bunny's fur,
Inside the bunny's fur, the crumb of a carrot,
Inside the crumb of a carrot, a strand of grass,
Inside the strand of grass, the bunny's blood,
Inside the bunny's blood, it's warm heat,
Inside the warm heat, the bunny's eye,
Inside the bunny's eye, sorrow,
Inside the bunny's sorrow, a speck of hope,
Inside the hope, a speck of reality,
Inside the reality, the sight,
Inside the sight, the bunny's tooth.

Max Taylor (10)
Rokeby School, Kingston upon Thames

Sensory Poem

It tastes like melted chocolate,
It feels like the softest mattress,
It smells like honey, just taken from a hive.
It sounds like water, rushing down as a waterfall,
It looks like melted gold.
I am your desire.

It tastes like soapy dishwater
With alligator blood mixed in,
It feels like a spiky wrecking ball,
It smells like milk left out for one thousand years,
It looks like a picture of Hell.
I am your worst nightmare.

Freddie Hamilton (9)
Rokeby School, Kingston upon Thames

The Hungry Snake In The Jungle

A colourful snake slid down a tree,
He hoped he did it silently.
If he didn't he'd scare his prey
And then his food would run away.
He saw a rat on the forest floor,
He slid, ate, but wanted more.
He saw another and with a smile of glee,
He slid towards it hungrily.

A fat snake sat on a branch,
He'd eaten well, he'd had his lunch.
Two fat rats were in his tummy,
Life in the rainforest is yummy, yummy, yummy!

William Goslett (8)
Rokeby School, Kingston upon Thames

This Lion

This lion's tummy is so fat
Because it's eaten a snack,
It ate a bat and a cat.
This lion's tail is as long as a child,
This lion's legs are one metre tall,
This lion is very scary,
This lion is very fierce,
This lion loves meat,
This lion's tail has a fluffy bit at the end,
This lion is very big.

Milan Patel (8)
Rokeby School, Kingston upon Thames

The Last Day Of My Life

On the last day of my life
I went on a walk with my wife,
Then I heard children play
In a strange little way.
Suddenly my heart turned black,
Like I'd had a little whack.
All of a sudden
My blood stopped.
The next day I was dead
In my little bed.

Alfred Grealis (10)
Rokeby School, Kingston upon Thames

The Cat And The Hummingbird

There was once a fat cat
That lay very still,
I even thought that it was ill,
Until a hummingbird came passing by,
Not recognising that cats lie.
The cat jumped really high
And caught the hummingbird in the sky.
The poor hummingbird let out a cry!

Daniel Francesco Merighi (8)
Rokeby School, Kingston upon Thames

The Fat Cat

The fat cat sat on the rat
Who lay on the mat
Which made a splat!
The fat cat and the rat sat on the mat
And the cat chased the rat round the mat.
Just then the door went rat-a-tat-tat
And in came another fat cat
And the little fat rat said, 'Drat.'

George Farago (8)
Rokeby School, Kingston upon Thames

Elements Of Freedom

Freedom is red, like the bright, beaming
sun shining down on you,
Freedom is an innocent child laughing,
like the joy it brings to your soul.
Freedom is a challenge, you will always have to fight for it.
Freedom is joy, because you fulfil joy when you have freedom.
Freedom makes you forget all your memories
because it clears your soul.

Max Benians (10)
Rokeby School, Kingston upon Thames

My Tortoise

My tortoise has a shell as big as a TV,
My tortoise has a head as big as a football,
My tortoise walks as slowly as a snail,
My tortoise is as big as a Monster Truck,
My tortoise has a nose as small as an ant,
My tortoise has feet as big as a large pencil case.

Freddie Laflin (7)
Rokeby School, Kingston upon Thames

Fun

Fun is yellow, like the sun,
Fun is a warm fire/ice cream smell,
Fun is yelling, like the children,
Fun is sweets like rainbows,
Fun is the ball being kicked like a rocket,
Fun is warm, like a campfire,
Fun is a reminder of children shouting.

Hyun Rang (10)
Rokeby School, Kingston upon Thames

Joy

Joy is happy, just like gold,
You can find it in the park, as it is told.
Joy's sound is just like laughter,
It is bigger than cheering and it is nicer.
It tastes like crumble that's really hot,
You can eat it with custard in a pot.
You can see it everywhere as long as it's nice.

Omaar Louis (10)
Rokeby School, Kingston upon Thames

The Shark

My shark is funny and he likes fish,
He is soft, warm and funny,
He is sneaky and naughty,
He swims fast and likes to swim,
He likes to chase fish for food,
He likes them, he says, 'They're very juicy!'
His teeth are sharp and he is blue.

Aaron Edmonds (8)
Rokeby School, Kingston upon Thames

Sadness

Sadness is grey, like rusty iron,
Sadness is like a creaky door in a mansion,
Sadness is horrible, like newborn maggots,
Sadness is pitch-black, like a stormy night,
Sadness is like a punch in the face,
Sadness is curdled, like gone-off milk,
Sadness is like the Grim Reaper.

Christian Levett (9)
Rokeby School, Kingston upon Thames

My Cat, Paws

My cat is as fast as lightning,
My cat is as fluffy as a carpet,
My cat's eyes are as big as Monster Truck wheels,
My cat is as naughty as a bee,
My cat is as playful as a fish,
My cat's ears are like satellites.

Christopher Arnold (8)
Rokeby School, Kingston upon Thames

The Summer

Kneel down and gaze -
Bride's veil, woven nylon?
No, just a glistening cobweb blowing
In the hot summer breeze.

Sit down and listen -
A song of peace and harmony,
A person playing the violin?
No, just a bird singing their everlasting song of joy
In the old oak tree.

Max Lloyd (10)
St Joseph's Catholic Primary School, Malmesbury

One Summer's Day

Crouch down and listen
Is it a children's choir?
No, it is just a bird singing
Tunefully like a flute
In an orchestra

Walk and feel
Is someone breathing on me?
No, it is just a summer breeze
Blowing like a fan
Cooling a classroom

Sit and smell
Is it someone's perfume?
No, it is just a summer rose
Drifting like the scent of an ice cream
On a summer's day

Stand and look
Is it a slick of oil?
No, it is just a dirty river
Flowing like a rough sea
Through the countryside.

Katie Kershaw (9)
St Joseph's Catholic Primary School, Malmesbury

Bad Is . . .

Bad is when darkness wraps around you
and curses all your heartbeats
like a devil in its lair.
Bad looks like a leopard ripping an unlucky deer to shreds.
Bad slithers down your bed
then makes you colder than a freezer, like ice.

Oliver Smith (9)
St Joseph's Catholic Primary School, Malmesbury

93

Recycle Our World, Look After All Things That Are Beautiful

Look around you,
Is it a toy, ready to be played with,
Or is it a painting drying in the sun?
No, just a wrapper someone just left there,
Lying trapped in a gate like a wounded animal.

Listen out for everything,
Is it an exotic bird singing a beautiful song,
Or a child singing a sweet song?
No, just the sound of the loud cars as they zip up and down the road,
Blocking out every other sound like a sound murderer.

Feel everything,
Is it the feeling of a warm hot-water bottle,
Warming you on a cold winter's night, or a soft blanket?
No, just the scorching sun blazing on our backs,
Burning us like a fire.

Freya Madeley (10)
St Joseph's Catholic Primary School, Malmesbury

Keep It Before We Lose It!

In the wind rattling crisp packets floating,
There's a strong smell, forcing you to smell it and get closer.
The long hose stretches out all along the path
Looking like a snake.
Birds sing powerfully to get some attention,
Waiting joyfully on the line.
The breeze blowing in front of you,
With the hot sun on your back.
Stepping through the gap,
Hear the crackling wood as you step.

Alexandra Kellogg (10)
St Joseph's Catholic Primary School, Malmesbury

Save It Before We Lose It!

Fall on your knees and stare -
A blue diamond, a gleaming moonstone?
No, just a common forget-me-not.
Scattered here and there like seeds in the wind,
Glowing in the soft moonlight,
Bright as the sun.

Step forwards and watch -
A red ruby, a green emerald?
No, just an English apple
Hanging like a bat off a branch.
Slowly spinning, shining in the sun,
Bright and happy.

Look up and listen -
Nightingale song, a choir from Heaven?
No, just a blue tit's song,
Drifting through the air like smoke
So beautiful and clear the deaf could hear it.

Emily Franklin (9)
St Joseph's Catholic Primary School, Malmesbury

Believe In Nature

Shush and listen -
An orchestra, a radio?
No, just a bird song,
from the bark-barren tree
ripe from the winter.

Look down and gaze -
An ice patch,
an oil spill?
No, just the weeds under
the water like a fishing net.

Alexander Alden-Fenn (10)
St Joseph's Catholic Primary School, Malmesbury

A Beautiful World

Eating fruit salad,
Under the lush pink blossom,
Staring at the lime-green leaves,
As circular as a bottle top.
Listening to the birds' repetitive song,
Leaping across rock pools.
Watching the fish dart around,
Like snakes in-between sand dunes.
Gazing at the pigeon doing his tightrope impression,
I caught the dandelion seeds,
Floating across my beloved green grass,
Sauntering across the stepping stones,
I caught a glance of the new tree,
A new summer,
A new chance,
A new life.

Abigail Charnock (11)
St Joseph's Catholic Primary School, Malmesbury

Because Of Pollution

Blooming in the summer air,
Of heat wave, I'm wilting
I smelt the fragrant perfume
Now I stink like a bin,
My bright luminous pink has gone,
I'm brown,
Come and they go,
My leaves have fallen,
I'm bending over like an old man,
Slugs and maggots
Gobble down my roots,
I'm fading away.

Georgia Conlan (10)
St Joseph's Catholic Primary School, Malmesbury

Stop And Think

As soft as velvet,
The cherry tree petals float softly to the ground,
Glistening summer grass,
Fills acres and acres of fields,
As sunny as the Caribbean,
As peaceful as Heaven,
Until . . .
I wake up!

As worn and torn out as last year's school shoes,
The trees stand bare,
Yellow and bristly grass,
Covers the last remains of nature,
Baby robins scream with hunger,
While their mother hunts,
For probably the last worm left.

Adeshola Sorungbe (9)
St Joseph's Catholic Primary School, Malmesbury

A Change

Dropping from the clear, colourful sky,
A robin loses its leftovers to the gentle Earth.
It splashes like water.
Roses explode as I jump past,
Petals shaped as hearts about to kiss you.

Litter hovers like dust,
As it drifts along the breathing air.
Some kill animals,
In horrible ways.
Soon it will be all over the place.
It won't be very nice for long,
If we carry on like this.

Saskia Harris-Neale (10)
St Joseph's Catholic Primary School, Malmesbury

Sunset, We Can Save The World!

The scarlet clouds warning,
When the sun's yawning,
Bluebirds pacing,
Pigeons racing,
The fresh flowers drooping
And the breeze looping.

The red traffic lights warning,
Busy drivers yawning,
The police warnings pacing,
Jet planes racing,
Some street lights drooping,
Trash looping,
In the air!

Paige Davy (11)
St Joseph's Catholic Primary School, Malmesbury

Hold Your Breath And Gaze!

Watch the sun as it goes around the world
With the scorching hot breeze
Wafting past you
Admiring the birds twittering and the pink blossom trees
Meanwhile whistling birds were balancing on a telephone wire like a
see-saw.

Save our world
Look after our world
And keep it clean.

Olivia Coletta (10)
St Joseph's Catholic Primary School, Malmesbury

The Prayer Garden

In the prayer garden,
The continuous orchestra of the blackbirds!
Grass whistles in the light breeze as the midday smell of roast fills
my nose with a luscious smell.

Oliver O'Shea (10)
St Joseph's Catholic Primary School, Malmesbury

In The Garden

In the garden,
The bird opera explodes with sound,
The pigeon tight rope walker trips and falls,
The ear-piercing robin screams its way out of the trees,
As the sky turns grey.

Joseph Dickson (10)
St Joseph's Catholic Primary School, Malmesbury

Bonsai Tree

The small Bonsai tree
Comes from Japan
Small, tiny, little
Leaves like green emeralds
Tree trunk like a cardboard tube
It feels like the start of new life
I feel gigantic in comparison
The small Bonsai tree
When was this created?

Ryan Crooks (9)
St Jude's RC Primary School, Fareham

The Old Forest

The old forest
Hundreds of years old
Misty, long and tall
Like trees twisting around me
As tall as Mount Everest
Like it's the best place ever
A magical place
The old forest
I'm the person that nobody likes.

Joe Nolan
St Jude's RC Primary School, Fareham

The Great Wall Of China

The Great Wall of China
Loads of people visit each year
Long, gargantuan, immense
As long as twelve double-decker buses
As long as fourteen thousand rulers
Glad we made it
I'd feel very short
The Great Wall of China
How long are you?

Ryan Garrard (10)
St Jude's RC Primary School, Fareham

The Magnificent Moon

The magnificent moon
You shine in the night
Big, round, bright
You look like a star in the sky
As beautiful as a pearl
You make me feel far away
You make me feel as small as an ant
The magnificent moon
You make me think of a big pearl floating in the sky.

Amielia Frances Adlington (10)
St Jude's RC Primary School, Fareham

The Ghost

The ghost's been haunting people for donkey's years
White, scary and ugly
Like a witch going to Hell
Like an angel going to Heaven
Like nobody's there
The ghost
The ghost scares me when he haunts me
I feel terrified.

Jack Dowie (11)
St Jude's RC Primary School, Fareham

The Bonsai Tree

The Bonsai tree
Comes from Japan
Tiny, beautiful and twisty
As fragile as a petal
Leaves as green as emeralds
It feels like your life keeps flowing
The Bonsai tree
When was this discovered?

Owen Walker (10)
St Jude's RC Primary School, Fareham

The Mighty Golden Gate Bridge

The Golden Gate Bridge
Approximately 749 feet tall
Huge, red and mighty
In the amazing city of San Francisco
As big as the glistening sea
As gold as the sun
The Golden Gate Bridge
How long does it take to paint you?

Ben Spelling (10)
St Jude's RC Primary School, Fareham

Football Stadium

Is a beauty to the world
Large, epic, fascinating
Like a field of crops
A wonder to the world
Like a flock of birds crowding like mad
It is a wonder to all that see it
Football stadium
Like a crowded beach.

Kieron James (11)
St Jude's RC Primary School, Fareham

The Ancient Cave

As old as God
Dark, creepy, rocky
As scary as you walking into a vampire
As dark as night
As scared as a rabbit getting eaten
Going into a vampire cave, scary
An ancient cave makes me feel like I'm having a lot of fun.

Jeffrey Jerome (10)
St Jude's RC Primary School, Fareham

The Perfect Pizza

The perfect pizza is very nice, thick or thin,
doesn't matter what.
It's every pizza put together,
ham and pineapple, meat feast,
pepperoni and cheese pizza.
And when you try this brilliant pizza
be prepared to be amazed.

Thomas Kingswell (10)
St Jude's RC Primary School, Fareham

The Huge Heaven

Lives in the clouds
Massive, sparkling Heaven
As peaceful as a dove
As calm as a lake on a summer's day
Where my grandad and nanny live
The huge Heaven
It reminds me of where we will all go.

Ben Colclough (10)
St Jude's RC Primary School, Fareham

A Wizard's Pocket

An exotic cheeseburger doing yoga.
A bag of mints and lollipops that last forever.
A multicoloured mouse that is always dancing the boogie woogie.
A bag of dust that makes boys turn into nuts for squirrels.
A green ball of fluff that gets bigger every time you cuddle it.
A swimming pool that changes colour every second.
A glass of water that's a swimming pool for an ant.
An iPod Touch that plays any song you can think of.
A giraffe pencil case that eats your pencils and pens.
A bag you must never open or you will turn to dust.

Elena Davis (10)
Sandon JMI School, Buntingford

What Is . . . ?

What is a koala? A cute and cuddly animal.
What is a spitfire? A spit of fire.
What is a fossil? A rock of history.
What is the solar system? A world of planets.

William Elkington (10)
Sandon JMI School, Buntingford

Mount Everest

Mount Everest
The biggest mountain in the world
High, tall, old
Like a giant ice cube
As big as the sun
It makes me feel small
Like a little beetle that no one can see
Mount Everest
It makes me feel cold.

Chiara Volpe (10)
Sandon JMI School, Buntingford

Seven Things Found In A Wizard's Pocket

A tissue as white as a cloud.
A rabbit as hairy as a furball.
A gobstopper you can suck forever.
Some spinning chips ballet dancing.
Mints as small as a little baseball.
A wallet as glittery as a party dress.
An iPod dancing in your pocket.
That is my wizard pocket, I hope you enjoyed it.

Eleanor Howard (10)
Sandon JMI School, Buntingford

The Egyptians

They lived in Egypt
Ancient, colourful, hot
As small as a ladybird
Hair as black as the sky
They make me feel tall
Like a big giant
The Egyptians
It's like I was there in history.

Joanna Simpson (9)
Sandon JMI School, Buntingford

What Is . . . ?

What is a flower? A sign of happiness.
What is water? Many lives.
What is magic? Many secrets.
What is an elephant? A friendly giant.
What is fashion? Something I don't know about.
What is a tree? A breath of life.
What are you? You.
What is the best way to finish? Like this?

Matthew Inman (9)
Sandon JMI School, Buntingford

What Is . . . ?

What is love? A relationship that never ends.
What is me? A kind, helpful kid.
What is a calculator? A mind-reading machine.
What is a lollipop? It's a sweet that never ends.
What is a heart? A world of love.
What is chocolate? A world of eating.

Shane McMahon (10)
Sandon JMI School, Buntingford

Ten Things Found In A Wizard's Pocket

100,000,000 purple puppies
A mouldy cupcake with blue sick for icing
A starry sky full of imagination
A loveable triumphant elephant
A giraffe doing a somersault
A fossil full of pre-historical history
A tissue the size of the world.

Lucie Payne (10)
Sandon JMI School, Buntingford

Seal

Silky flipper
fatty blubber
fur coat wearer
pups lover
ocean swimmer
energy manufacturer
ice sitter
quality diver
squid eater
shark as a predator
what am I?

A seal!

Georgia Kirk (10)
The Leverton Junior School, Waltham Abbey

Turtle

Shell wearer
Massive egg layer
Green coater
Slow mover
Plastic choker
Jellyfish eater
Ninja fighter
What am I?

A turtle.

Ben Humphreys (10)
The Leverton Junior School, Waltham Abbey

The Magic Box
(Inspired by 'Magic Box' by Kit Wright)

In my box I will put . . .
Six sizzling, scrumptious sausages
Purple sky
And three Mount Everests.

In my box I will put . . .
A wondrous dream and an old tatty shoe
Some whipped cream
And a second Christmas.

In my box I will put . . .
Chunky, chewy chocolate caramel
A pink chicken
And a china cup.

In my box I will put . . .
A screaming soul, a wicked witch
A dancing tree
And the unexplored universe.

Joseph Chaleyssin (10)
Town Farm Primary School, Staines

Playground Riddles

I am long and thin,
I come in outstanding colours,
I sometimes come big and sometimes small,
I am entertainment to play with.
What am I?

I bounce when you throw me,
Usually I'm quite tiny but I'm smashing to play with,
I come in lots of colours,
Sometimes I'm mixed colours.
What am I?

I am made out of tough wood,
Everyone loves playing on me,
People are delighted to have me in their playground,
I'm enjoyable to play on.
What am I?

Everybody plays on me,
I'm bright and green,
Animals amble through me,
You can cut me.
What am I?

I'm always there if you are in trouble,
I'm helpful and kind,
I give out gold slips,
I tell people off if they are naughty.
What am I?

I'm circular shape,
I come in many colours,
I am used by going round people's hips,
Mostly girls like to play with me.
What am I?

Grace Toms (10)
Town Farm Primary School, Staines

The Sea

As I sprinted to the sea,
An enormous wave jumped into the air
And landed on the lumpy rocks,
I then tasted some sea salt
And then I felt contented.

I could see all marvellous things,
I could see, I could see,
Lumpy rocks on the sand,
The bright sun in the bright blue sky,
The dolphins jumping up and down in the blue sea.

The sea, the sea,
I could hear, I could hear,
The crashing against the rocks,
The sea, the sea,
I could touch, I could touch,
The sea, the wind, the rocks and the water,
The sea, the sea.

I can smell,
The sea salt and the bright sun,
The sea, the sea,
I can taste, I can taste,
The sea salt,
And the lovely, blue, sparkling water,
The beautiful sea.

Tilly Aimee Gartlan (10)
Town Farm Primary School, Staines

The Playground

Who's in the playground?
What can I see?
A shaggy old bee.

Who's in the playground?
What can I hear?
I can hear a really loud TA screaming
at a little pupil in goofy old way.

Who's in the playground?
What can I touch?
I can touch a really sore scar
on my really terrible skull.

Who's in the playground?
What can I smell?
I can smell a really bad stench
on my really bad bench.

Who's in the playground?
What can I taste?
I can taste not a single thing
because there is no food in my playground base.

Who's in the playground?
What can I do out there?
Stay out there of course
you silly old bear.

Oliver Ellery (10)
Town Farm Primary School, Staines

Riddles

I'm usually green or brown
Lovers lie around me and so does grass
You skip on me and you can dig me
What am I?

I am a spherical shape
I come in different sizes and colour
I normally am black and white
You can break windows with me
What am I?

I'm like jelly, I come in different sizes
You throw me
I have different colours
I have liquid inside me
You have fun with me
What am I?

I come when there's rain
I'm grey and people hate me
I normally live near mountains and French people
Call me Illiadaiobrozlad
What am I?

Apenisa Tanuku (10)
Town Farm Primary School, Staines

What Am I?

I come in different colours,
I can come in all sizes,
I can be as light as a cup,
I like being kicked around,
I like boys playing with me.
What am I?

Gbemisola Ogunfiditimi (10)
Town Farm Primary School, Staines

The Playground

I hate the playground,
Do you?
No one plays with me,
I feel annoyed!

I like the playground,
Do you?
Everyone plays with me.

I hate the playground,
Do you?
I always fall over.

I like the playground,
Do you?
I never fall over.

I hate the playground,
Do you?
The football always gets kicked at me.

I like the playground,
Do you?
The football never gets kicked at me.

Joshua Geary (10)
Town Farm Primary School, Staines

Football

It's round like a sphere,
black and white hexagons,
the ball is round like the Earth,
the ball is hard and light,
kick, kick, *goal!*

Daniel Stokes (9)
Town Farm Primary School, Staines

The Playground

You can climb on me
And you can play on me
Jump on me
What am I?
  Climbing frame.

I am sometimes yellow or orange
I can give you a tan or a burn
What am I?
  The sun.

I am green and shiny
Sometimes wet
What am I?
  Grass.

I am good for racing on
You can use me whenever you want
What am I?
  Racing track.

Shania Brown (9)
Town Farm Primary School, Staines

What Am I?

I am hard
I am soft
You use me in games
What am I?

I am any colour you like
I am any shape you like
You can do anything to me
I am not waterproof
What am I?

Mollie Carlisle-Smith (9)
Town Farm Primary School, Staines

Playful Playground Riddles

I am colourful,
I am used by boxers in training
What am I?
Rope.

I am colourful, round and hard,
Some famous people like John Terry use me.
What am I?
Football.

I am green and fluffy,
People like Andy Murray use me.
What am I?
Tennis ball.

I have got soft juicy leaves,
Spiders scatter down by brown bark.
What am I?
Tree.

Sinead Nicolaides (10)
Town Farm Primary School, Staines

The Playground

Possible children playing with ties
Land ahoy to the toy
Apple cores on the floors
Tears, tears, always dropping on my ears
Never fear Lucy's here
Gold, gold shimmering, glimmering, glinting gold
Rice, rice, tasted nice
Up, up and away
Oaga, oaga skidilya, it's a lovely woodchuck day.

Lucy McEwen (9)
Town Farm Primary School, Staines

Birds

The skies are quiet,
the birds are hiding,
hiding like a fox,
waiting for the right time,
always peeping, never looking,
waiting, waiting, always waiting,
the birds are getting ready,
never looking behind,
nearly there, almost now.

Now the birds are flying,
flying very high,
the big, burning, blazing hot sun,
beaming in their eyes,
they keep on flying,
they find the right place to land,
landing, landing, landing, landing anywhere.

Rhyannon Hughes (9)
Town Farm Primary School, Staines

The Playground

In the playground I can see
lots of children running round me.

In the playground I can see
lots and lots of pretty bees.

In the playground I can hear
the space aliens chewing what's near.

In the playground I can taste
I can taste fish paste.

In the playground I can smell
the fresh scent of my auntie Mel.

Luke Billett (10)
Town Farm Primary School, Staines

The Outstanding Playground

The playground is amazing
It's really fun to play in
I can see some friends to play with me.

The playground is amazing
It's really fun to play in
I can hear the birds of prey
Singing while I play with clay.

The playground is amazing
It's really fun to play in
In the playground I play with the skipping rope
I know I do.

The playground is amazing
It's really fun to play in
I always play with my friends
Right until the very end.

Sharna Harmes (10)
Town Farm Primary School, Staines

Footballs In The Playground

Round and bright coloured
Big and small
All the sizes
Score the goal
Black and white
Little hexagons
I have black spots
and a white ball.

Callum Peel (9)
Town Farm Primary School, Staines

The Playground

Who's in the playground except for me
And my little bumblebee?
Aliens and animals, flowers and leaves.

Who's in the playground except for me
And my little bumblebee?
Teachers playing tennis, running round a track.

Who's in the playground except for me
And my little bumblebee?
Flowers and leaves on a tree.

Who's in the playground except for me
And my little bumblebee?
No one looking after me
Except for my little bumblebee.

Tanesha Dodd (10)
Town Farm Primary School, Staines

The Playground

In the playground
the bins are smelly.

In the playground
the swings are high.

Children like to play
children like to eat.

In the playground
the jungle gym is fun.

Children screaming
children laughing.

In the playground
it's so much fun!

Chloe Standley-Williams (10)
Town Farm Primary School, Staines

Playground

I am thin, long
You can cross with me
What am I?
 Skipping rope.

I am soft
You can play on me all day and night
What am I?
 Grass.

I am made of wood
You can stand on me
What am I?
 Trim trail.

Ben Porter (10)
Town Farm Primary School, Staines

Animals!

Animals are cute little things,
they have big eyes and chubby cheeks,
they're furry and very colourful,
they can be short, tall, small and low,
they're meant to be Man's best friends,
they're a lot of money to keep,
people love them and they're very playful, fit and healthy,
watch out, they're troublemakers sometimes!

Jemma Wild (10)
Town Farm Primary School, Staines

My Magic Box

(Inspired by 'Magic Box' by Kit Wright)

I will put in my box . . .
the first chocolate bar
and the ghost of the last emperor of ancient Greece.

I will put in my box . . .
the first flower
and a scrummy sausage.

Amber Williams (10)
Town Farm Primary School, Staines

Football

It's round like a sphere
Black and white hexagons
The ball is round like the Earth
The ball is hard and like lightning.

Charlotte Darby (10)
Town Farm Primary School, Staines

Toby's Poem

T oby, full of laughter.
O ranges are my favourite fruit.
B ubblegum smile and full of fun.
Y ou make my life a better place.

Toby Williams (10)
Town Farm Primary School, Staines

Joy

Joy is like a fluffy cloud in your head.
Joy is like in the bath with the jelly bath.
Joy is like the pitter-patter of money.
Joy is like looking into a cool freezer.
Joy is like tasting white candyfloss.
Joy is like smelling my baby brother's head.

Saffron Rivers (7)
Whatfield CE (VC) Primary School, Whatfield

Cow

Maid dressed in black and white,
Gives a dog an awful fright.
Mostly when it's dark at night,
But a harmless beast when it's light.

What am I?

Ebony-Brooke Rivers (10)
Whatfield CE (VC) Primary School, Whatfield

Peace

Peace is the opposite of war,
Peace tastes like chocolate,
Peace sounds like silence,
Peace looks like treasure,
Peace smells like the perfume called 'Ghost',
Peace feels like a soft pillow.

Shaun Mitura (9)
Whatfield CE (VC) Primary School, Whatfield

Fun

Fun is the sound of children at the funfair.
Fun is running on the sand at the beach.
Fun is when you eat a chocolate doughnut.
Fun is looking through a sweetie shop window.
Fun is smelling the steak cooking in the frying pan.

Jade Samuel (7)
Whatfield CE (VC) Primary School, Whatfield

Silence . . .

Looks like eating pudding
Tastes like pure air
Smells like an old book
Sounds like a preying mantis
Feels like a feathery duckling.

Billy Cotter (9)
Whatfield CE (VC) Primary School, Whatfield

Joy

Joy is going swimming.
Joy is having a little girl.
Joy is having some ice cream with my best friend.
Joy is having a best friend.

Maisie Cotter (7)
Whatfield CE (VC) Primary School, Whatfield

Love And Anger

Love

Love is like a golden wedding ring,
Sliding on the bride's 4th finger.

Love is a warm cuddle
As the bright yellow sun
Shines down on you.

Love is like walking into a colourful sweet shop
As you chew up the apple bonbons you bought.

Love is a white dove
As it sings in an apple tree.

Anger

Anger is like a black bomb
Ready to explode into a million pieces.

It fills the air with grey smoke
As everyone smells the burning wood
On the bonfire.

Anger is like ash spitting out of the fire
And onto your sleeve,
Ouch, it burns.

Anger is like an angry wasp
Flying round your ear
Making an annoying buzzing noise.

Dawn Poole (10)
Witnesham Primary School, Ipswich

Guilt

Guilt is black, like in a cold, dark, lonely room, on a cold winter's day.
Guilt is brown, like you're trapped under a wooden bowl
for the rest of your life!
Guilt is red, when your face turns red and rosy because you know
you're guilty but can't spit it out.
Guilt makes you feel tense and nervous.
Guilt is when you know you're the one to blame and it makes you feel
lonely, worried and sometimes confused.
Guilt tastes like out-of-date rock, so hard you can't get into it
(it nearly breaks your teeth!)
Guilt tastes like hard crusty bread.
Guilt smells fishy, like someone's lying.
Guilt smells like frying onions soaking in their own fat!
Guilt is wrong!

Lauren Whiting (10)
Witnesham Primary School, Ipswich

Anger

Anger is the colour of black darkening the room.
Anger is the colour of red, red as dark as blood.
Anger smells of the burnt ash coming out of a fire.
Anger smells of smoke choking everyone.
Anger tastes like a burning sausage out of a barbecue.
Anger makes you feel like stomping around breaking anything
in your path.
Anger feels like getting shot by a pistol.
Anger looks like a poor village after a hurricane.
Anger looks like a thunderstorm striking buildings with its powerful
electric bolts.
Anger sounds like crashing of cymbals and booming of drums.
Anger sounds like a slamming door about to fall off its hinges.

James Poole (11)
Witnesham Primary School, Ipswich

Winning

Winning is the colour gold ,when you are handed the gold medal.
Winning is the colour yellow, as the dandelions grow in the grassy meadow.
Winning is the colour blue, because you're tired after the race of glory.
Winning is the colour red, because your cheeks are ruby after the race.
Winning is the colour green, because the trees were cheering for you to win.
Winning is the colour orange, as the warmth of the sun shines on you.
Winning is the colour silver, as the judges hand you the trophy.
Winning is the colour pink, as confetti sprinkles on you.

James Phillips (10)
Witnesham Primary School, Ipswich

Love

Love is crimson, like red roses given on Valentine's Day,
it is also the pale pink of the confetti thrown in the air at weddings.
There is the smell of love at weddings,
of the freshly laundered dresses trailing on the ground.
The smell of love is also a heart-shaped box with chocolates in,
waiting to be opened.
Love tastes like a dinner for two by candlelight,
in addition love tastes like chocolate sundaes,
lovingly prepared on a sunny afternoon.
Love feels like you're on top of the world
and that nothing can go wrong.
Love looks like a happy couple holding hands.

Faye Gooch (11)
Witnesham Primary School, Ipswich

Shocked

Shocked is the colour of many vibrant colours bursting into one.
It smells of sour sweets and a shimmer of sour smells.
Shocked is the taste of burning, hot, fizzy drinks tingling in your mouth.
Shocked feels like spiky thorns pricking you and an exciting feeling tingling down your back.
Shocked looks like a big, spiky, colourful ball that bounces vibrantly all the time.
Shocked is the sound of shouts and screams crowding round a market stall.
Shocked is like many coloured flashing lights all at once that blind you.

Max Williams (10)
Witnesham Primary School, Ipswich

Love

Love is the feeling like on a sunny day.
Love is red, like a rose bush.
Love smells like chocolate cake baking in the kitchen.
Love tastes like happiness in the air.
Love feels like my heart beating fast inside my body.
Love feels warm when I look at a newborn baby.
Love is when you walk down the aisle on your wedding day.
Love is yellow, like the sun beaming down on the glass.
Love smells like sweets in a large jar.
Love tastes like a kiss.
Love looks like a red heart.

Lauren Watling (11)
Witnesham Primary School, Ipswich

Guilt

Guilt is grey, like a cloud in a thunderstorm, pushing down,
building up the pressure.
Guilt is black, like a bomb waiting to go off, you know it's going to
happen but you don't know when.
Guilt is dull blue, like a rainstorm, you feel gloomy until it has
stopped.
Guilt is black, like a spooky night, you just want it to be over.
Guilt is brown, like a dodgy sweet, you wish you hadn't eaten it.
Guilt is black, like a monster sucking out all the happiness in your
life!

Charlie Boast (10)
Witnesham Primary School, Ipswich

Anger

Anger feels red, like a raging bull
Anger feels black, like a thunderstorm
Anger sounds like a lion's roar
Anger sounds like a rumbling storm
Anger tastes like revenge
Anger tastes like boiling water
Anger looks like a raging fire
Anger looks like an active volcano
Anger smells like hot coals
Anger smells of burnt wood.

Ben Jepson (10)
Witnesham Primary School, Ipswich

Anger

Anger is red, like the eyes of a raging bull charging at a cape.
Anger is black when it surges through you, blocking your senses.
Anger is black, like a feeling of pure hatred.
Anger smells red-hot, like a raging fire reducing something to dust.
Anger tastes like red-hot chilli peppers, which burn in your mouth.
Anger is like a black surface burning hot in the sun.
Anger is black, like the eyes of a snake.
Anger is grey, like a bullet zooming through the air,.
Anger is bright, like a howl of pain.

Blayn Bosworth (11)
Witnesham Primary School, Ipswich

Disappointment

Disappointment is as white as snow, like dying but not.
Disappointment smells like warm cocoa.
Disappointment tastes like tears low on your cheek.
Disappointment feels like someone taking away your bow from the arrow.
Disappointment feels like you've been working on a flower then it perishes like bread dough.
Disappointment sounds like a person crying.

Edward Lacey (11)
Witnesham Primary School, Ipswich

Happiness

Happiness is bright yellow, like the sun.
Happiness smells like sweet strawberries being eaten.
Happiness sounds like children laughing as they play in the street.
Happiness feels fun as you run up and down the running track.
Happiness tastes fantastic, like joy in the air.

Kirsty Goodchild (10)
Witnesham Primary School, Ipswich

Guilt

It is dark as it overcomes your body.
It tastes like salt as you hide away.
The sound of a thousand voices shouting out the truth.
It feels like you are bubbling with darkness and about to blow.
It looks like the door to escape keeps getting further and further
away.
The truth explodes out and with a sigh of relief you feel better.

Harry Hogger (10)
Witnesham Primary School, Ipswich

Sadness

Sadness is black like a funeral of one of your loved ones.
Sadness is like a thunderstorm,
the rain tears of the unhappy clouds.
Sadness tastes bitter like the juice of a lemon.
Sadness is like the sound of tears,
the falling and crying of young and old people.
Sadness feels like rain soaking my clothes right through to my skin.
Sadness can sometimes scar people for life.

Azareah Foster (10)
Witnesham Primary School, Ipswich

Happiness

Happiness is like a rainbow gleaming in the rain
Happiness is cheerful and brings peace to the world
Happiness tastes sweet, like a bowl of strawberries and cream
Happiness is yellow, like the sun beating down
Happiness is red, like the poppies on the grass
Happiness is blue, like a peaceful river lapping against the rocks
Happiness is green, like trees blowing in the wind.

Meghan Thorneloe (9)
Witnesham Primary School, Ipswich

Anger

Anger is red, red like blood.
Anger is blue, like the sea's crashing waves.
Anger is red, like a hot blazing fire.
Anger is black, like a brewing storm.
Anger is red, the colour bulls charge at.
Anger is yellow, like a bolt of lightning.
Anger is red, like an angry heart.

Alexander Craggs (11)
Witnesham Primary School, Ipswich

Anger

Anger is red, like the cape with a bull charging towards it.
Anger smells like smoke as it surges through your body.
Anger tastes like red-hot chilli peppers burning your insides.
Anger feels like a fireball raging around inside you,
stopping you from thinking.
Anger looks like a raging tsunami, destroying everything in its path.
Anger sounds like a deafening roar, like thunder on a stormy night.

Robert Doig (11)
Witnesham Primary School, Ipswich

Happiness

Happiness is all bright and colourful like a rainbow in the sky
Happiness tastes like a sweet fizzing in your mouth
Happiness feels like the warm sun beating down on you
Happiness is like a smiling family
Happiness sounds like laughing children.

Joe Burnard (11)
Witnesham Primary School, Ipswich

Love

The colour of love is red, like a rose.
It smells like blossom.
Loves tastes like lipstick.
Love looks gruesome and makes you feel sick.
It feels great.
I love it.

Jamie Lea (9)
Witnesham Primary School, Ipswich

Young Writers Information

We hope you have enjoyed reading this book - and that you will continue to enjoy it in the coming years.

If you like reading and writing poetry drop us a line, or give us a call, and we'll send you a free information pack.

Alternatively if you would like to order further copies of this book or any of our other titles, then please give us a call or log onto our website at **www.youngwriters.co.uk**.

A platform for your poetry!

Young Writers Information
Remus House
Coltsfoot Drive
Peterborough
PE2 9JX
(01733) 890066

Get in touch!